• NATIONAL ARCHIVES OF INDIA •
ARCHIVES IN INDIA HISTORICAL REPRINTS

A TOUR IN THE PANJAB AND RAJPUTANA IN 1883-1884

• NATIONAL ARCHIVES OF INDIA •
ARCHIVES IN INDIA HISTORICAL REPRINTS

A TOUR IN THE PANJAB AND RAJPUTANA IN 1883-1884

H. B. W. GARRICK

UNDER THE SUPERINTENDENCE OF

ALEXANDER CUNNINGHAM

What the learned world demands of us in India is to be quite certain of in our data, to place the monumental record before them exactly as it now exists, and to interpret it faithfully and literally.

James Prinsep

GYAN

Published by

Gyan Publishing House
5, Ansari Road
Daryaganj, New Delhi-110002
Phone: 011-47034999, 9811692060
E-mail: books@gyanbooks.com

Distribution Network
gyanbooks.com
India, USA, Canada, UK, Australia, France

ISBN : 978-81-212-4131-1 (PB)
First Published, Calcutta, 1887

2nd Impression 2020

Printed at: Gyan Press, Delhi.

Archæological Survey of India.

REPORT

OF

A TOUR IN THE PANJÂB AND RÂJPÛTÂNA

IN

1883-84.

BY

MR. H. B. W. GARRICK,

ASSISTANT ARCHÆOLOGICAL SURVEY OF INDIA,

UNDER THE SUPERINTENDENCE OF

GENERAL A. CUNNINGHAM, R.E., C.S.I., C.I.E.,

DIRECTOR-GENERAL OF THE ARCHÆOLOGICAL SURVEY OF INDIA.

VOLUME XXIII.

"What is aimed at is an accurate description, illustrated by plans, measurement, drawings and photographs, and by copies of inscriptions of such remains as most deserve notice, with the history of them so far as it may be traceable, and a record of the traditions that are preserved regarding them."—LORD CANNING.

"What the learned world demand of us in India is to be qnite certain of our data, to place the monumental record before them exactly as it now exists, and to interpret it faithfully and literally."—JAMES PRINSEP.

CALCUTTA:
PRINTED BY THE SUPERINTENDENT OF GOVERNMENT PRINTING INDIA.
1887.

VOL. XXIII. **PANJAB AND RAJPUTANA.** PLATE I.

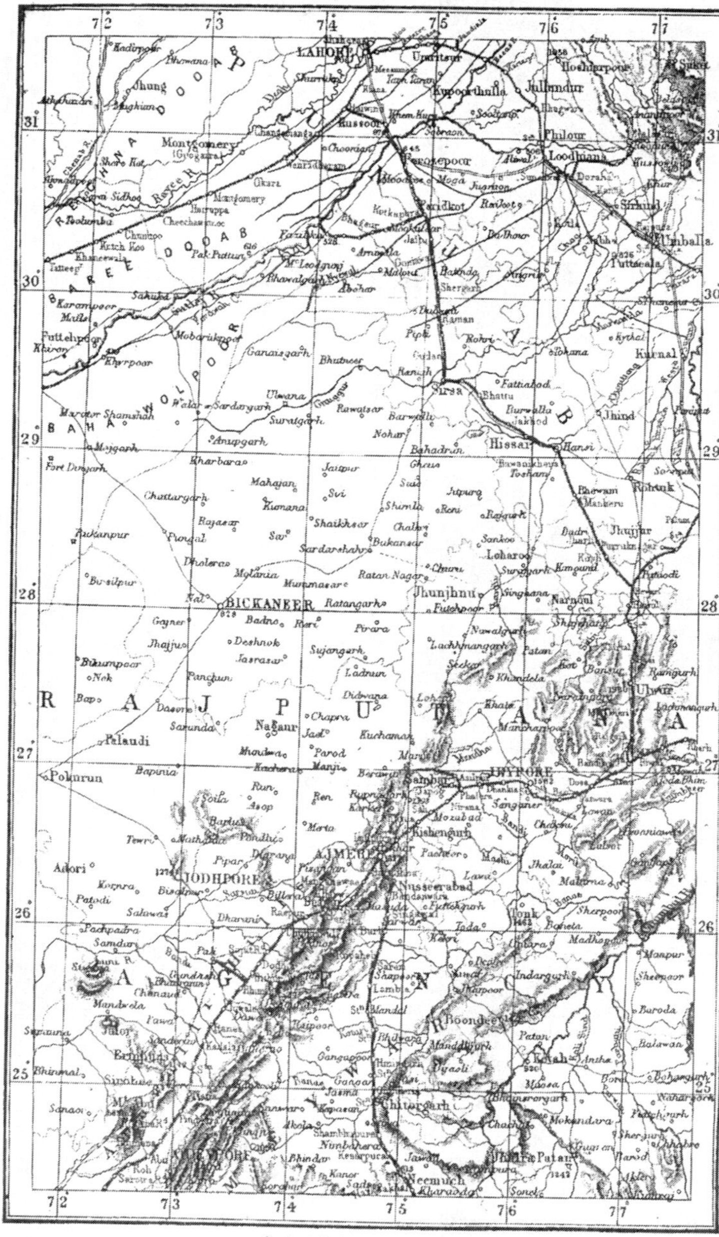

Scale 1 Inch = 64 Miles.

Printed at the Survey of India Offices, Calcutta, December 1886.

PREFACE.

DURING the past field season, my work laid for the most part in Eastern Rájpútána, and included some of the southern districts of the Panjáb.

Leaving Simla on the 1st of October 1883, I examined the ancient forts at Bhatinda, Sirsár and Hánsi, together with the mosques and monolith of Firúz Sháh Túghlak at Fattehábád. The next place of importance on this route is Túshám, celebrated for its rock-cut Gúpta inscriptions, of which I secured photographs. A quantity of inscribed *data* was also collected at the old sites of Hánsi, Bairát, &c.; it is to be regretted that the Asoka inscription at the latter place is almost entirely effaced, and does not lend itself to reproduction by mechanical means; I conclude, however, that it is merely a transcript of Asoka's edicts, of which so many copies are found incised on rocks and boulders in Northern India.

From Bairát my route passed through Amba and Jaipúr (the old and new cities of the Kachhwahas) to Ajmir, after a short halt at which place I marched across the Indian desert to Nágor or Nágapúri, an ancient site in the Márwár State, hitherto unexplored; and which contains, amongst other interesting objects, some fine temples. In this neighbourhood I came in contact with the desert tribe of Sahárias, who are said to be of Arabian extraction, and take their tribal name from the Desert of Sahára; of this tribe, and likewise of the Sondhias, I prepared an ethnographical account in a separate paper.

I next visited Mandor and Jodhpúr, the old and new capitals of Márwár, peopled by the Rahathor refugees from Kanoj; and crossing the Aravali range of mountains at Komalmir, descended into Náthdwára, a very sacred site in the Meywár State, and proceeded thence to the Great Sisodia Fortress of Chitor, where I made photographs and impressions of various inscriptions, including those on the "Tower of Victory" (*Jaya Stambha*), which have been inaccurately translated by Tod.

The past year's tour extended southwards to Nimach, and terminated at Agra on the 31st of March 1884. Much difficult country has been traversed; twenty-nine old sites explored, and twenty-eight drawings and photographs prepared within the limits above indicated.

H. B. W. GARRICK.

CONTENTS.

PLATES AT THE END OF THE BOOK

ARCHÆOLOGICAL SURVEY OF INDIA.

REPORT OF A TOUR IN THE PANJÂB AND RÂJPÛTÂNA IN 1883-84.

1.—PÎR KHÂNEH.

THERE is but little of archæological interest in, and about, the line of country directly south of Lahor, until Bhatinda is reached, and the following few objects, so far as my information goes, are the most noteworthy on either side of the ground watered by the Sutlej river between Bhatinda and Lahor.

First, comes Pîr Khâneh, which is the name given, collectively, to a group of old Muhammadan buildings, including two tombs of the Ghorean period.[1] Numerous faqirs and dervishes use the place more as a monastery, or common rendezvous, than anything else, for little or no attention is paid to the *manes* of the entombed *Pîrs* who give their name to this spot.

As my stay here was only of one day's duration, I could not make any but a superficial examination of the Pîr Khâneh, nor was it necessary to delay in the neighbourhood of Shergarh, as Pir Khâneh is only a representative, though on a notably large scale, of several such establishments in this part of India, where, save these Musalmân relics, no old architecture is to be seen. But this paucity of ancient monuments can be accounted for when it is borne in mind that a large section of the population is composed of Sikhs, who, unlike the more eastern Hindûs, are a new sect and require few establishments

[1] The Muhammadan rulers of this period had the affix of Ghori to their names, derived, it is believed, from their habit of hunting the wild ass *Ghorî*.

for worship; hence the *Gûrûdwârâs* are few and far between. I believe there is no Sikh monastery of this description between Sirsa and Thalvandi. The people make pilgrimages to either place annually—indeed, one sorely misses in the Panjâb the goodly Brâhmanical establishments and architectural examples so plentiful elsewhere.

2.—BAKHTU.

About ¾ mile north of Bakhtu is a largish and unevenly shapen mound, or *tibâ*, strewn in nearly every part with broken brick and pottery, much of which is of a dark or black colour: some moulded fragments were also found here, but too much mutilated (especially the bricks or tile specimens) to make out any connected pattern from. Coins also are, I am told, found during, and directly after, the seasonal rains.

This *tibâ* is generally of a circular form, and extends over 20 bighas of ground. It is cultivated in several places, but the ploughs hitherto employed have not, strangely enough, struck upon any decided walling. But, in spite of this assurance of the villagers, I am convinced that this mound marks the site of an ancient city of some magnitude.

In the total absence of all local tradition, it is impossible to account for the origin of the Bakhtu mound, and the people in the adjacent village of Shergarh also professed ignorance as to the present whereabouts of any of those medals, &c., they at first informed me it had yielded; some, however, said that they were generally made over to the district authorities.

3.—TIRANDA, BHATINDA (BHATI-DA-NAGARA OR GOVINDGARH).

The first object seen on entering Bhatinda from the north is the massive and lofty fort now called Govindgarh, which name it lends to the straggling little town (an outpost of the Patiâlâ State), erst *Tiranda* and *Bhatinda*. Besides being the *first*, this fort certainly is the *foremost* feature here; and before proceeding any further with this account of the place, I will endeavour to give the results that attended a careful inspection of this building, in which inspection I was much assisted by the *Kill'ahdâr*, or "Governor of the Fort," who courteously showed me all over his trust.

The walls of this edifice are extraordinarily massive, and built with the usual slope; being 53 feet at base and 35 feet at summit in thickness, and 100 feet high. The most perfect *bûrj*, or "bastion-tower," is exactly 120 feet above the ground-level of the town which surrounds the fort.

In plan Govindgarh proper is a square of 686 feet, with 32 small and 4 large bastions, of which the former are arranged 8 to each side (the building faces the cardinal points) and the latter 1 to each corner. These large bastions are 291 feet in circumference at top; but the minor towers are much smaller.

Some time ago the walls of this fort encompassed a small village which was imprudently built upon, or near to, the powder magazine; but since this exploded and removed the inhabitants more violently than was good for them, no one lives there excepting the sentries and *Kill'ahdâr*, whose dwellings being in the gate and main circumvallation respectively, they stand in no danger of a similar catastrophe. The only gateway is in the eastern face, but placed in the northern end of that face, and the fort is surrounded by a mud or *dhûs* wall, of 1,300 feet side and 14 feet thick; but measured across from the edge of its battlements (of which there are twelve to each face), 43 feet in thickness. But these outworks, though comparatively modern, being erected since the possession of this fort by the Patiâlâ State, are much dilapidated and only traceable in a few places, of which the most perfect are towards the west, north, and south; indeed, I doubt if these extramural works *ever* existed on the east side, where the town approaches very near to the main walls of the fort, in the centre of which are the remains of a tank, 86 feet square and 26 feet deep, surrounded by four brick walls, 43 inches thick. The tank is approached from the south by a *pakka ghât*, or brick floor, suitable for bathers; but it is at present quite dry and out of use.

The fort of Tiranda is locally said to be 1,800 years old, and to have been built by *Râjâ Dab*, an ançestor of the celebrated *Vena Pâl.* Though I found several small *Lakhowr* bricks of comparatively modern make throughout the building, these were probably used in additions, or repairs, of which it has undergone many; and the large bricks, which were in parts, leave little doubt that this edifice existed long prior to the first Muhammadan invasion.

The general appearance of the fort exteriorly is solid, plain, and rather ungainly in its block-like and angular outlines. But, owing to its excessive height, it is seen from several miles all round, and travelling along the northern road from the Sutlej, I sighted the building from a distance of 7½ miles.

There is a tradition at Bhatinda to the effect that the same masons who built this fortress also erected the similar castle at Bhutnair, and hence I am tempted to look to the first syllable of either name for the etymology of that of this early site. That Bhatinda owes its name to the Bhatti race we have the authority of tradition, besides the rather contradictory account of Colonel Tod, who in *Râjasthân*, Vol. II, page 179, says—

"[1] Bhatnair, which now forms an integral part of Bikaner, was anciently the chief abode of another Jât community, so powerful as at one time to provoke the vengeance of kings, and at others to succour them when in distress. It is asserted that its name is in no wise connected with the Bhattis who colonised it, but derived from the Bard or Bhat, of a powerful prince, to whom the lands were granted, and who, desirous to be the founder of a poetic dynasty, gave his professional title to the abode. In the annals of Jessulmer, it will be seen that there is another story accounting for the appellation, which recalls the founding of Carthage or Byrsa. Both legends are improbable; and the Bhats' annals confirm what might have been assumed without suspicion, that to a colony of this race Bhatnair owes its name, though not its existence.

"The whole of the northern part is called *Nair* in the ancient geographical nomenclature of Maroothah, and when some of the Bhati clans became proselytes to Islâm they changed the vowel *a* to *u*[2] to distinguish their parent stock, *viz.*, Bhatti for Bhutti."

[1] It should be borne in mind that this was written in 1814.

[2] Here the first *a* is evidently intended to be pronounced long, as *Bhâtti*, and the *u* as the short unmarked *a* generally used in transliteration into Roman character, and not as the *â* long of modern transliteration.

With the preceding extracts, which are themselves professedly extracts from indigenous works on Bhati history, I will close my remarks on these people, and, having ascertained who the Bhattis are, revert to the subject which called for those brief remarks,—*i.e.*, the etymology of *Bhatinda*.

Bhatti-da-nagara, or "the Bhatti's city," was, in all probability, the full form of this name, originally from *Bhatti*, the tribe, and *da*, largely used in the province as the genitive particle in lieu of *sa* or *ka*, of which it is merely a dialectic variation. Of the habit of omitting the final word *nagara* or *pûra* (which merely signifies "town" or "city") and retaining the sign of the genitive case, numerous examples exist in which such terminations are *understood*, and the intermediate nasal may or may not be employed; indeed, the word is often pronounced by the people *Bhatida*, seldom *Bhatinda*, and *never Bhâtinda*, with the long vowel, so that it cannot possibly be derived from *Bhât*, "a bard," nor from anything save *Bhatti*, a title by which apostate Hindûs embracing Islâm are generally known; and, consequently, the name cannot be older than the eleventh century, when the Mòslems from the West carried their arms across the Sutlej, creating shoals of "true believers" *en route*, and it would appear that their most numerous converts were recruited from the *Yadûvansa*.

Of this *vansa*, or "race," was the renegade *Bâbâ Hâji Rattan*, who, according to local tradition, besides forsaking the religion of his sires, betrayed his master King *Vena Pâl*, whose minister he was, and for these two estimable qualities, in addition to a pilgrimage (*hâj*) to Mecca, the mausoleum of *Bâbâ Hâji Rattan* is now venerated as that of a saint! This tomb is situated half a mile east of *Govindgarh*, or "Fort of Govind," a Vaishnav name, compounded from *Govind*, "Lord of the Cow," one of the titles bestowed by the cowherds of *Vrij* upon Krishna, and *garh* or *gad*, "a fort." Around this principal *roza* of the sainted *Hâji* are grouped five smaller tombs; these are built of brick, facing the south, and are inscribed in parts by lines of Arabic writing—apparently quotations from the Qorân—worked into the stucco in relief, but so much has been broken away that comparatively little can be read. *Yâ-rahmân* opens the legend on the larger tomb, which, after a cry for mercy, thus begun in the Hâji's name (and not by any means unnecessary, if tradition correctly records the sum of his iniquities), exhibits the *Hijri* date 309, and this is the date of the Hâji's death. In the book written by command of *Shahab-ûd-din Ghori* this date is, however, contradicted, for here—*Ser-ûl-mutâkhar-in*[1]—the demise of *Bâbâ Hâji Rattan* (who commenced building his tomb in *Hijri* 700) is placed in 722 of the flight; and to the munificence of His Majesty "*Kha-khân*" is assigned the grant of a monthly stipend of 1,111 rupees to keep these tombs in repair. We are also informed in this volume that the sum was paid to the son of the Pîr, but if we are to judge from the present appearance of these buildings, this fund must have long ceased to exist. But there are other, and much later, records of donations for repairs in and about these tombs, of which we will give those on four *kûtbas* situated outside, and to the north of the enclosure, as the only ones decipherable. On the first is preserved merely the name of *Lodar-mal* with the *Hijri* date 1002; on the second we read, "*The respects of the humble slave Badi Chand, father of Girdhâr Mal, of the Fort, Muharram 1033 H.*" On the third: "*Repaired by command of Nawâb Jabar Khân, by the hand of Sheikh Khâdim, in the commencement of Ramzân the auspicious, 1011 H.*" On the 4th: "*Repaired with chunâ* (lime) *and kalai* (mortar) *by order of the humble Nawâb Shâhdâd Khân, by the hand of Khûdim Muhammad Afzal* (probably the mason), *Zilhij, 1131 H.*"

These records are principally interesting on account of the large proportion of Hindû names which they exhibit as having contributed towards the repairs of Musalmâns' tombs, but they only bear fresh testimony to the wholesale apostasy formerly practised by the Hindûs of these parts.

It is said that the name of "Bâbâ Hâji Rattan" was adopted by the popular hero of Bhatinda after his conversion to the faith of Islâm, with which religion he is said to have

[1] A MS. book which I obtained in the neighbourhood of Hujrah, and which is in my possession.

become fascinated about the period of Shâhâb-ûd-din's invasion, at which he, as the minister of Râjâ Vena Pâl, connived, rendering the Moslem every assistance to enter the fort and put his master and the royal family to the sword. The original, and Hindû, name of this elder was *Chankar*, and that of his father *Kânwar Pâl.* "Highly educated in the arts and sciences, he (Bâbâ Hâji Rattan) embraced Islâm, and making a *hâj* (pilgrimage) to Mecca, became a Hâji." (*Ser-ul-Mûtakharin*, p. 384.)

From the names in the following genealogical table, it will be seen that the descendants of this renegade retained his adopted faith :—

Genealogy of Kânwar Pâl and Bâbâ Hâji Rattan.

Kânwar.
|
Chankar or Bâbâ Hâji Rattan.
|
Dâud.
|
Tâj Muhammad.
|
Shaikh Muhammad Afzal.
|
Allah Bakhsh.
|
Muhammad Raushan.
|
Rattan Bakhsh.

Besides its undoubted antiquity, Bhatinda has witnessed some thrilling scenes within the last eight centuries, for it was here that Gogga, the famous Chohân, fell, after being driven back from his defence of the Sutlej against the invading Musalmâns; here also Jaipâl was captured, but the hero of Ghazni only found the king of Lahor lifeless, for the fort of Tiranda had just witnessed the suicide of that fugitive chief, who preferred death to the foreign yoke. There can, however, be little doubt that multitudes followed a less violent, if less glorious, course than did Jaipâl, and, like the local hero and saint, Bâbâ Hâji Rattan, *alias* Chankar, chose to bend with the necessities of the times, and, like him, forsaking Hindûism, became proselytes to the new faith and consequently Bhattis. Should this etymology for *Bhatinda* be accepted, we have also the *period* of its substitution for *Tiranda*, the older name of this interesting site.

But more interesting still is an inscription of nineteen lines on a stone slab of the Gûpta period.[1] This inscription, until December 1880, was concealed in a corner of the inner vault, or *sanctum sanctorum*, of Bâbâ Hâji Rattan's tomb. In December 1880 it was, however, discovered by Sir Robert Egerton, K.C.S.I., the late Lieutenant-Governor of the Panjâb, then on a visit to Bhatinda, and conveyed by His Honour to Lahor. By subsequent enquiry I learnt that this inscription was handed over before its discoverer's departure from India, to Sirdâr Attar Singh, C.I.E., Chief of Badhaur, to whose kindness in sending me the stone I am indebted for the photographs and impressions I have been able to secure. In an account which appeared in the Urdû Patiâlâ paper shortly after the discovery of this tablet, it is said to contain *twenty* lines, of which the only readable letters "seem to be हहर्ति"! whereas the letters, excepting those near the centre, which appear to have been ground down by some means, are in fairly good preservation, and, were it not for the unfortunate fracture which deprives us of quite a third of the record, it would be easily decipherable. So much for native journalism.

Besides the objects above mentioned there are at Bhatinda, 1st,—*Sûrkh Bhavâni*, an early Hindû building; 2nd, *Mira Sâhib's Qabar*, in which there is an old Persian inscription, in which I read the Hindû title *Mâharâja* (مہاراجہ), but the name, with the rest of this record, is entirely defaced. In the *Chamâr's tola* hard by is a circular and irregularly formed *bûrj*, much venerated by the lower castes; also another round *bûrj* near the fort.

4.—SIRSA OR SIRSE-PATTAN.

To the south-west of Sirsa is situated a large ancient fort, which is about 3 miles in circuit, but of so irregular a form as entirely to preclude the possibility of detailed measurements being made; indeed, the whole resembles in

[1] The letters here appear to me somewhat modern for Gûpta characters. See Plate XXVII.

appearance a mighty irruption. This lumpy mass is divided, near the centre, by a trench-like hollow, running east and west, and this depression is said to mark the situation of the division which, in olden times, existed between the city and the fort—a very plausible theory in its way, for one portion (that called the site of the ancient fort) is considerably higher than the other, upon which the city is said to have formerly stood. The general height of these remains cannot be less, and is probably more, than 75 feet above the surrounding fields.

On the very summit of this mound I found a solitary tomb of white marble, elaborately inscribed, much broken, and rapidly sinking below the surface of the ruins upon which it stands. It is unknown who is interred here, but a general belief exists that the mortal remains of a *Saiyid*, who conquered this fort, rests within the vault. I have, in my collection of impressions, the Arabic inscription, which contains merely extracts from the Qorân, though very ornamental and apparently old, carefully arranged and joined together in the position it occupied on the stone of this tomb.

By the intelligent natives of Sirsa and its neighbourhood, this fort is assigned to the third century A.D., and therefore is as old as anything in this part of India. There is a popular tradition which seeks to account for the name of this city as follows: It is said that a recluse was once interrogated by a band of pilgrims as to the correct name of the site, when in reply, he said, *Kabî Sirsa, Kabî Nîrsa*, *i.e.*, in the local dialect "sometimes extant, sometimes extinct," from *nir* or *nira*, "is not;" and this is said to have particular reference to the countless wars then being waged for supremacy, as the country in those disquieted times is reputed to have been alternately inhabited and laid waste no less than twenty-one times. But this derivation is contested by another tradition, which derives the name "*Sirsa*" from the former profusion of *Sirsa* or *Sirisa* (*Acacia speciosa*) trees here; the name was anciently *Sirsepattan*.

In the *Gûrûdwâra*, or Sikh monastery at Sirsa, are preserved some interesting Sikh relics, which were found enclosed in an iron box, in some excavations lately made at Haripûr. These relics comprise a papyrus or birch bark manuscript of the Sikh prophet and religious leader. The purport of this document, which is written in Gûrûmûkhi, is an exhortation to fervent and constant devotion, and a promise, under the seal and signature of the *Gûrû*, to manifest himself to devout worshippers. It is dated V.S. 1756, or A.D. 1700, and appears to have been written with a brush, or very broad stilet, in a brownish ink or colour. There are also some fragmentary inscriptions and a small white marble *bas-relief*, representing a pair of diminutive feet; this is called *Gûrûpâd*,[1] and is much venerated by the attendant Sikhs and worshippers at the establishment.

To the *sarovar* or *sarwar*, "tank," north of this Gûrûdwâra, great antiquity is assigned, and it is stated that this tank is unfathomable, and that it was excavated in V.S. 315, or simultaneously with the erection of the ancient fort of Sirsepattan. The walls of this tank are very massive and built of large bricks; the southern wall clearly runs *underneath* the Gûrûdwâra building, and I was told by those to whom the most reliable information concerning the subject should be accessible, that there are seven subterraneous passages, or caves, leading from the tanks' wall, or embankment, to the fort. At the time of my visit to Sirsa these caves were, however, invisible, on account, I was given to understand, of the water in the tank being then too abundant, but at low water the entrances to these caves are said to become apparent.

At Sirsa there is also a Town Hall, in front of which there is a pleasant garden, with a fountain. In this Town Hall building the authorities have displayed further sculptures, discovered at the Haripûr excavations, and, if I understand aright, at other diggings lately made at the Sukandpûr ruins, which are quite close to Sirsa and which I visited. Amongst these sculptures may be mentioned an ably-executed group, in reddish sandstone, of Indra and his consort, mounted upon an elephant. This piece is 2½ feet high, though the figures are deprived of their heads. A larger statue here is the figure of Vishnu, attended by two votaries, which measures 4 feet high.

[1] The "Teacher's foot-prints."

The most remarkable of several architectural fragments in this hall is an elaborately-carved square base of a column, 1′ 1½″ in diameter. There are, besides, perforated and carved trellises, screens, &c., in white marble, exhibiting designs, both floral and geometrical.

In the country between Sirsa and Rania further west, there are altogether four *theas*, or *tîbâs*,—*i.e.*, mounds bearing signs of former occupation. The first, or more easterly, of these mounds is situated about 1,000 paces west of the village of Ûttû, or about one march west of Sirsa. This deserted site still preserves its ancient and modern names,—*i.e.*, *Thikri-wâli thea Râm nagaria* and *Fatteh-pûr*. Second, at two marches west of Sirsa, is a nameless mound containing large boulders suitable for building purposes and *débris*. The third is a small mound close to Bhatnair, from which some coins are said to have been exhumed about four years ago. The fourth, and oldest, *tîbâ* is situated 2½ miles south of Rania (between Ferozâbâd and Rania), and this measures nearly 250 feet long, but is of very irregular shape.

The existence of all these remains, together with several others which I saw, but which are too small to notice here, may be taken as proof of the antiquity of this locality. Few bricks are, however, anywhere found, and thin shales, or chips of stone, seem to have formed these now-forgotten habitations; pottery, too, is thickly strewn over all the sites above indicated.

5.—FATTEHÂBÂD.

In the spacious courtyard of a mosque at Fattehâbâd stands a fine column of red sandstone, inscribed with the genealogy of the Tughlak emperor Feroz-shâh, in beautifully-formed *túghra-Arabic* characters carved in high relief. This inscription extends right round the pillar, and, defaced as it is towards the south, has been translated by Maulvi Ziyauddîn Khân, Khân Bahâdûr, Extra Assistant Commissioner. For a general view (from the east) of this pillar, see Plate II.

Besides the *lât* at Fattehâbâd, there is an inscription, also in high relief, of Humâyûn on a slab of compact, light-yellow limestone, measuring 2′ 3½″ long by 1′ 5½″ broad, and sunk into the screen-wall of the mosque, immediately behind, or to the west of the *lât*.[1] Another inscription, on a slab 3′ 4″ long by 8″ broad, is let into a wall to the north of the pillar and first inscription, and merely bears *intakhâb Qutbas*, or extracts from the Qorân.

The latest mosque here is a modern structure built by one Khair-ûd-dîn, lambardâr. This is not an ungraceful building, in, we may say, the latest style of Muhammadan architecture, being erected but sixteen years ago. It is the tallest building in Fattehâbâd, which town owes much to this mosque on the score of external appearance.

But the most interesting building in Fattehâbâd is that called *Muhammad Humâyûn Bâdshâh ka Masjîd*, an exquisitely proportioned and enamel-decorated little mosque, and evidently the oldest here; for it is said that that romantic Mughal emperor, of chequered career, on his flight to Amarkot, passed through Fattehâbâd on a Friday, and, hearing the *muazzin's* call to prayer, ordered a halt, with a view to pray in this mosque, which has since borne his name. The inscription of Humâyûn before mentioned was originally found in this building and removed to the large mosque-screen where it was discovered by me. For a view of this mosque see Plate IV.

The site upon which Fattehâbâd stands, and indeed the neighbourhood for miles around, is said to have originally been the *shikârgâh*, or "hunting-grounds," of Northern India, and densely wooded and stocked with the largest game: were this not universally affirmed by the most enlightened natives here, it would be difficult to credit, as this neighbourhood is particularly barren just now. But similar instances of the total disappearance of forests are not scarce,—*e.g.*, the Yûsafzai plains, where the founder of the Mughal dynasty used to hunt the wild elephant, and where now a single tree is seldom seen.

It was while on a hunting excursion with his sons that Feroz-shâh determined to reclaim a portion of this forest, and fixed upon this site for a town which should be called Fattehâbâd, after Fatteh Khân, his favourite son. Having four sons,

[1] See Plate III.

however, it became necessary to found, in all, four towns ; three more spots were accordingly chosen, on which a similar number of townships were in due time built and called after these remaining princes, as follows: *Jaffirâbâd* after Jaffir Khân, *Rajibâbâd* after Rajib Khân, and *Muhammadpûr* after Muhammad Khân. The last-named three places are now mere villages, or ruins, and not comparable with Fattehâbâd.

6.—HÂNSÎ (ASA) OR AMBA.

There is much diversity of opinion regarding the origin of this city, and many theories are abroad amongst the people of *Hânsî*—the first and most generally believed hypothesis being that *Anang Pâl Thanur* founded it ; 2nd, that *Râja* (or *Rai*) *Pithora* was the founder ; 3rd, that *Asa*, the *Jât*, conquered and proclaimed himself king of the citadel, calling it after his own name, Asa, which, by the dialectic modifications of succeeding ages, has become Hânsî. I also found that the place had, at one period of its history, been called *Ambir*, or *Amba*, for which name tradition accounts in this wise: Ambanâth, a son of the Chohân Râjâ, was indisposed when the king brought him to recruit his health to this place, and upon his son's recovery he in gratitude excavated the tank, built a fort, and founded a city, calling it by his son's proper name, *Amba*. The Settlement Report has still another version, assigning this foundation to *Mânik Rai Chohân*.

On the ancient and extensive mound which represents the old fort of Hânsî there is the *dargâh* of the saint, or *Wâli*, *Hazarat Saiyid Shâh N'iâmat Ulla*,[1] who, in 559 of the *Hijri*, accompanied *Sultân Shahâb-ûd-dîn Ghorî* in his victorious attack upon this fort, and on this spot lost his life in battle, becoming, in consequence, a *shahîd*, or martyr; and his descendants still enjoy some free land and divers other privileges accorded by Government. At the site of this tomb, a *mêlâ*, or fair, is held every March, at which much charity is dispensed. A regular guard of *mûllahs* is entertained to tend this tomb, and thus one, at least, is always to be seen dusting

[1] See Plate V.

or hunting away flies from it; separate brushes of peacocks' feathers being kept for both these purposes. This *khângâh* is visited by Muhammadans, and even by certain classes of Hindû pilgrims, who could not possibly be more reverential were it that of the prophet Muhammad himself. At the entrance and in the interior of this *khângâh* are two Arabic inscriptions, dated in H. 593 and H. 953 respectively. Of these I have transcripts and impressions, and also of the inscription with which the tomb of the commander Hazarat Saiyid Shâh N'iâmat Ulla is surrounded. These letters, worked into high relief in the stucco ground, have, I was given to understand, been thrice restored since their original composition, but in no wise altered. The tomb has an imposing appearance, which is not lessened by the prostrated pilgrims paying homage to the departed warrior; these pilgrims almost cover the floor (*mussallah*) of this *rozâ*, and the ornamented cloth with which the tomb is covered is regularly changed and held down by white marble carpet slaves. It is a difficult matter to get admitted within this holy *rozâ*; but, happily, the good *mûllahs* are fully awake to their own interests, and hence it is not impossible.

Equally interesting are the old Muhammadan tombs on the west side of the city. Of these, one building or vault contains the remains of *Kûtb Jamâl-ûd-dîn*, better known as *Chahâr Quṭb*, whose father was *Sûltân Jamîd-ûd-dîn*, who came from the west, and, along with the renowned warrior Shahâb-ûd-dîn Ghori, conquered this country in H. 558. After this conquest Hânsî fell to the share of *Quṭb Jamâl-ûd-dîn*, when, it is said, the Quṭb withdrew from the affairs of Government, and, preferring retirement and religious devotion, became a disciple of *Hazarat Bâwâ Shaikh Faridganj Shûkrpâk* of *Battan* or *Pattân* (? Pâk Pattan). The religious example of *Quṭb Jamâl-ûd-dîn* was followed by *four generations* of his descendants, and hence his name, or rather title, *Chahâr Quṭb*. In H. 670 Quṭb Jamâl-ûd-dîn died, and his tomb, before mentioned, is very handsome and forms a columnated dwelling for countless *darvishes*.

Near to the above *rozâ* is a large *masjid* containing four inscriptions which set forth some important local names (the largest of these records are dated in H. 876 and 623, respectively), of all of which I have careful and complete copies, and some of which I have partly read. I have also a transcript of the dated stanza on the great *Barsi* gate of the city. I was assisted in making all these transcripts by competent local *mûllahs*, and have endeavoured to collate some of them in order further on. Nearly all the inscribed data at Hânsî contain notable historical and local names, and the collection I obtained is rather large—some of the best inscriptions being found in the meanest and least likely looking tombs.

The principal inscriptions at Hânsî are as follows:—

1st.—On the door of the shrine of Hazarat Saiyid Shâh N'iâmat Ulla—"*25th of month of Rajab, 696 A.H.*"

2nd.—On tomb—"*Shrine of 'Ali, son of Asphandzâr, 10th of Zilhaj, 593 A.H.*"

3rd.—"*In praise and gratitude to God, Raza 'Ali, 903, erected outside of the city this shrine of Hazarat Quṭb Jamâl-ûd-dîn, son of Sûltân Hâmid-ûd-dîn, who came with Shahâb-ûd-dîn from Ghazni and conquered this part of the country. The city of Hânsî having fallen to his share, Hazarat Quṭb Jamâl-ûd-dîn became a recluse, and was the disciple of Hazarat Bâwâ Shaikh Faridganj, of Pâk Patan. He died in A.H. 670. His shrine* (hazira) *is pure, handsome, and in contiguity with a mosque.*"

4th.—The following is the inscription on the above-mentioned mosque: "*Built in the name of God, and in the reign of Bâdshâh Muzaffar, son of Mubârik Shâh, one of the pious and great, by the hand of Shaikh 'Abdûl Fatteh, a disciple of Shaikh Jamâl-ûd-dîn, to whom may God give a place in heaven. Whosoever may pray here should remember him in their prayers. The writer of the inscription is Roza Quli, resident of Hânsî, Mohulla Zuhdujan, in the Mohurram 877 H.*"

5th.—On the wall of mosque—"*With the aid of God.*"

6th.—Near door of ditto—"*Hazarat Quṭb Sâhib. The door of Rahmat Gilâni of Masûd-ûd-Ispahânî, whom may God assist.*" From which I infer that this door was built by, or at the expense of, this individual from Persia.

7th.—Not legible.

8th.—On a pointed arch—"*Hazarat Shaikh Jalál-úd-dín Muhammad Sáhib*" (not legible) "*In the time of Allah-úd-dín Abú Muzaffar Sháh Jahán Muhammad Sháh—may he reign for ever—was built this door on the 10th of Rabi-úl-Akbar, in the year 703 H.*"

Inscription of Dini mosque—"*With the aid of God and Hazarat Muhammad Mustafa (the Prophet) was built this mosque, on the date of Zil. Haj. 767, in the time of Feroz Sháh*" (Tûghlak?).

9th.—Inscription of Buali Bakhsh mosque—"*Built by Ahmad, son of Muhammad Asmandi, in Rabi-ul-Akbar 623.*"

There is also a dome on the shrine of Hazarat Qutb Jamâl-ûd-dîn, but it has no inscription, although I found a fillet which appeared well adapted for such. It is just possible that this building was never thoroughly completed.

The most beautiful tomb here, and one of which I secured a photograph, is that of the merchant *'Alam*,[1] who is said to have been the *Mir-tajarah*, or Chief Purveyor or Farmer-General, of Sultân *Jámid-úd-dín*. The façade here resembles, in no slight degree, one of our own minsters, if we could imagine the intricate and beautifully preserved design to be wrought in stained glass, instead of charmingly arranged pottery.

This example of glazed tile work surpasses, in the freshness and harmony of its colouring, anything I have yet seen, not excepting the first specimens at Mûltân and elsewhere, and the vault is certainly one of the very first that underwent this process of embellishment, when the art of burning these tiles was in its early purity; for, in later examples, I have always remarked performances distinctly inferior both as to harmonious arrangement and permanency of colour. Regarding the latter quality it will scarcely be credited that these fresh and brilliant tints have withstood the effects of nearly 700 summers, yet such is the case.

The canopied tomb, here called the *chhatri*, is also a fine, though comparatively small, structure, in red sandstone

[1] See Plate VI.

This building is said to be the oldest monument here of the Muhammadan period, and contains a large vault, besides inscriptions, which, however, are unfortunately defaced and incomplete.

The sepulchre of the merchant *'Alí* or *'Alam* (who is also called the *mûrîd*, or disciple, of *Qutb Jamâl-ûd-dîn*) measures 137 feet in total circuit, allowing 34′ 3″ for each face, as the building is quadrangular, and 46′ 9″ high. The walls of this beautiful mausoleum are 6′ 3″ thick; hence the inside area is 22′ 10″ clear each way, and the lower vault contains nine tombs (see Plate VI).

The square canopied tomb (locally called *chhatri*) is 43′ 4½″ in circuit, or about 10′ 10″ across, each face being also square, and 17′ 10½″ high. Four carved sandstone pillars support the enamelled canopy, and the vault contains two graves, said to be the oldest in Hânsî.

The oblong canopied building measures 39′ 3″ long, 8′ 7½″ broad, and 17′ high. The canopy rests upon ten ornamented columns, and the building contains eight graves of Qutb Jamâl-ûd-dîn's descendants, two of whom were themselves *Qutbs* (see Plate VII).

The large *masjid*, which has before been mentioned as containing so many excellent inscriptions, measures, from its northern to its southern extremities, 60′ 6″, and 33′ 1″ east and west; the walls of this imposing edifice (which is about 50 high) are 4′ 6″ in thickness.

The most important of the early Musalmân architectural remains in the fort of Hânsî are enclosed by an irregular circumvallation, which measures 89′ east and west, 81′ 7″ north and south, 35′ high, and its walls vary in thickness from 4′ 5″ up to more massive dimensions. This is no continuous or regularly-designed wall; on the contrary, its existence owes quite as much to chance as to the architect, for the enclosure is composed almost entirely of ruins and a feeble attempt, long since abandoned, at wall-building apparently intended to shut out the vulgar from the sacred *rozâ*, as these tombs or mosques are collectively called. The south portion of this walling is most picturesque, and here the tottering ruins, which hang together in a wonderful manner, at once form an arched gateway and house the *mûllahs* of the establishment.

The remaining objects inside the *rozâ* consist—

1st,—of a large *Ghorean masjîd* measuring 43′ north and south, and 23′ east and west. The walls of this elegant building, which is moderately high and contains some fine inscriptions, are 5′ in thickness;

2nd,—a smaller, and apparently more modern, *masjîd*, measuring 33′ north and south, and 15′ 6″ east and west, or 97′ in total circuit, and having walls 6′ 3″ thick. The style of this building is not unlike some others here, and must be of a much later date than those already briefly described.

Outside the enclosure I found two richly-carved columns of the water-vase or *kumbha* shape, 5 high, and, from the design of their overlapped capitals (a modification of the earlier "bell finale"), I conclude they must be old. By a comparison with General Cunningham's article on the subject (*vide* pp. 88-89, Vol. X, Archæological Survey Reports) these pillars would appear to belong to the third decade of the Gûpta bell-shapen capital characteristic of early Hindû architecture, and may, therefore, be assigned to the fourth or fifth century A.D. Along with a small figure frieze inside the *rozâ* enclosure, these pillars are the *sole existing relics* of the Hindû period on the fort-mound, and are pronounced by the people, who are intolerant Moslems, to be fragments belonging to the reign of the *kâfir Rai Pithora;* they did not know of their existence before I found them, and seemed to regret that they had not been destroyed along with all the other *bûts*, or "idols." These beautiful pillars at present serve the humble purpose of supporting the *charsâ* apparatus of a deserted well, which was thickly overgrown and almost hidden from view by dense *jangal.* They were evidently taken from some long-since-demolished Hindû temple whose very foundation cannot now be found, and which probably belongs to a time even long prior to Rai Pithora himself, to whom every thing of Hindû origin is assigned, and from whom the local hero and saint,

Hazarat Wâli Saiyid Shâh Ni'âmat Ulla, in company with Shahâb-ûd-dín Ghori, is said to have captured the fort, &c.

Outside the *khângâh*, or *rozâ* enclosure, is the isolated tomb of Saiyid Karim-ulla Sâhib, a pupil of Hazarat Wâli Saiyid Ni'âmat Ulla; this tomb measures 57′ in circuit.

The fort of Hânsî itself resembles, in more than one respect, that of Sirsa, though it is not so high as the latter, and appears to be of more modern construction than the Sirsa fort. The moat-remains here are visible in several places, and one approaches the fort from the city side through a massive gateway, apparently a modern addition. The excellent preservation of the winding ramp and general condition of this fort render it almost fit for present use.

Near one of the city tanks are ten small Hindû shrines; but these are quite modern.

7.—TÛSHÂM OR TOSHÂM.

The great Toshâm rock, upon the eastern face of which is built the populous town which bears its name, is situated 16 miles to the south of Hissar, and is the most remarkable natural feature on the face of these plains. Quite visible from Hânsî, this tall mountain of stone, upon a closer acquaintance, and viewed from the north, assumes precisely the form of a quantity of grain poured from a measure on to a flat surface; indeed, such a heap of grain would probably exhibit more irregularities in its conformation than do the two (east and west) sides of this huge rock. These two sides rise out of the ground-level curving gradually inwards (concavo-concave) in exact unison with each other until the apparently conical summit of the rock is gained; this summit is not, however, really conoidal in form, as an ancient fort, resting on an artificial plateau, surmounts the rock, and it is to a somewhat distant and strictly northern view of the Toshâm rock that my remarks are at present confined.

The important chain of hills of which the Toshâm rock may be called an isolated link, is very carelessly—not to say wrongly—laid down in some of the maps I have seen, and in others they are not marked at all. This mountain process may be described as a disjointed chain of rock eminences running nearly north and south, each principal rock sheltering, as it were, a village or town, which is invariably called after the rock nearest to it; thus (beginning from the north), 1st, *Khanak-pahâr* shelters the village of Khanak; 2nd, *Dudâni-pahâr* shelters that of Dudâni; 3rd, *Saral-pahâr*; that of Saral; and, 4th, *Negâna-pahâr*, that of Negâna.

Again, a less regular chain of rocks, which may be described as a series of isolated links, or out-riggers, of the first chain, runs a similar course, but further to the east. These rocks, counting from the north, begin with—1st, *Tûshâm-pahâr*, which shelters Toshâm; 2nd, *Dharam-pahâr*, which shelters Dharam; and, 3rd, *Rewâssa-pahâr*, which shelters Rewâssa. The *patra*, or "plateau," of light sandy soil, out of which these remarkable rocks rise, with the aid of very little water, bears fair crops of *bajra*.

There are distinct traces of *ancient* fortifications from the foot to summit of the Toshâm rock. According to the Settlement Report of the Hissar district, Râja Amr Singh of Patiâlâ "erected a fort at Tûshâm;" but, if this is the case, the Râjâ could have done little more than *restore* or *add to* the already existing fortifications of this ancient site, which are assuredly much older than the period of this prince. At present these fortifications—whether they have been restored or not, and probably they have been often restored—are in ruins, though clearly traceable. The general entrance, or ascent, to this hill fortress appears to be from the west, where a rampart, built of large, partially-dressed stones, with two tiers of steps, is visible. This was probably an outpost, for nothing further exists till the outer circumvallation, or *safil*, of the fortress is reached. Having been in disuse for so many years, the ascent is difficult and somewhat dangerous; but to trained mountaineers it presents, even now, a ready thoroughfare.

I have already stated that these works are assuredly old, and this will not, I think, be disputed when it is known that the ordinary size of the bricks of which they are constructed is nearly *a yard in length* (I found several examples, measuring 2′ 9″ × 2′ 1″ × 2½″), and that the rock-cut *baolis*, or "water reservoirs," here are not of the kind fashioned by moderns: moreover, it is, at least, unusual to find decayed caves of recluses, *mûnis* or *bhikkhus*, attached to modern structures, and all these objects are proper to the ancient hill fortress of Toshâm.

On reaching the summit of this rock an irregular plateau, covered with a vigorous growth of jungle, presents itself; also some structural remains, the most clearly apparent of the latter being the main wall towards the east-by-south corner, and nucleus of one of the towers, which seems never to have been finished or carried any higher than its present elevation, as I found some very old *chabûtras*, or cubic platforms of stone—apparently used for seats—on the top of it. There are, besides, seven *kûnds*, some of which, at the time of my visit, contained a small quantity of water. These reservoirs are called and situated as follows: The larger one, inside the fort, appears to be nameless; but the remaining six, situated mostly along the eastern brow of the hill, are, commencing with that furthest to the south, called *Pandûtirtha*, or "the pilgrimage of *Pandû*;" *Sûrya Kûnd*, or "the sun tank;" *Nasla*, *Kûnd*, *Kukar Sarovar*, and *Giâsa Kûnd*. A Musalmân sepulchre composed of a large heap of rough boulders, and situated to the east of the rock, is called *Bâbâ Farîd ka Khângâh*.

Before taking leave of the great rock of Toshâm, I will mention that the most interesting of its many interesting features is an ancient inscription of the Gûpta period,[1]—that is to say, the characters here incised belong to an epoch between A.D. 164 and 224, according to General Cunningham's computation. This valuable antiquity is situated on the eastern aspect of the Toshâm rock, into an overhanging facet of which it is incised.

Somewhat more than half-way up the rock, this inscription is difficult of access and particularly difficult to copy, especially by means of photography; but, by taking advantage of some peaked rocks overhead, around which ropes were passed

[1] For a general view showing the position of this inscription, see Plate VIII and for a photograph of the inscription, see Plate XXVII.

and tied to the photographic apparatus, &c. (which may be said to have *hung against* the lower rocks), I contrived to get a good record of this important inscription, of which I also took an inked and pencilled impression; the latter is, however, very unsatisfactory, owing to the extreme roughness of the stone upon which the writing is engraved: indeed, so shallow and indistinct have the letters become by the action of rain, &c., that they appear to assume distinctly different forms at various times of the day, or declivities of the sun; and it was not without several unsuccessful trials that my photographs were obtained.

The following are the readings hitherto obtained of this principal inscription.[1] They are from mere impressions, and, if any are inaccurate, may hereafter be amended from my photograph. (See Plate XXVIII.)

"No. 1 inscription in large characters consists of a single line—

"'*Jita Bhagavato bhakti chatur dise.*'

"'May the worshippers of Bhagavata increase throughout the four quarters.'

"No. 2 consists of the word *Achârya*, or 'teacher,' written twice in large characters.

"No. 3 appears to have been intended for a repetition of No. 1, but the only portion now legible is *Jita Bhagavata.*

"No. 4 consists of three lines—

"'*Gautamasa gotrena Râvanya putrena Achârya Achala bhatta threna.*'

"'Written by the descendant of Gautama, the son of Ravani, the teacher Achala bhatta.'

"These four inscriptions are later by one generation than the longer and more neatly executed record No. 5, as the name of Rawani is the last in it, while No. 4 is a record of her son.

"No. 5 inscription consists of eight lines, of which the first two begin more to the left, and are somewhat larger than the rest. Below the middle of the inscription there is a sun standard, exactly similar to that which is found on all the gold coins of the Gûpta king Ghatotkacha, who probably reigned from about 50 A.D. to A.D. 79. The inscription is certainly as old as the time of the later Indo-Scythians, as the form of the letter *n* is earlier than that in any of the Gûpta inscriptions. Indeed, the name of Ghatotkacha himself is found in

[1] Arch. Rep., Vol. V, pp. 138-140.

the beginning of the second line, but the inscription is not a record of the Gûpta king himself, but of his conqueror, the Tushâra king Vishnu, which was engraved by a Buddhist mendicant named Imama.

"For the following translation and notes I am indebted to the kindness of Bâbû Pratapa Chandra Ghosha, the learned Librarian of the Asiatic Society of Bengal:—

"*Line 1.*—Let the (halo) arising from the lotus face of Jambavati protect the Bhikshu Imama.

"*Line 2.*—By the frost of Vishnu (or by Tushâra Vishnu) the glory of the lotus face of the ladies of Ghatotkacha.

"*Line 3.*—Many people uninvited, Aryas, followers of Vishnu, professors of the Yoga philosophy.

"*Line 4.*—The great-grandson of the faithful in Bhagavat Yasatrata, the grandson of the professor Vishnutrata.

"*Line 5.*—The son of Vasu Deva, born of Ravani, the grandson of Sravama, professor and teacher.

"*Line 6.*—Of (*Pa*) dmagatanaya, professor, giver of opinion (or counsel) of the . . . feet of Bhagavata.

"The first record in line 1 is doubtless the name of the Buddhist mendicant, or Bhikshu, in whose favour protection is sought. The word *ava*, 'protect,' is the verb.

"In the 2nd line, Vishnu is evidently the name of a hero or king, who, having conquered Ghatotkacha, causes the face of his enemy's wife to be downcast, poetically whose frost causes the lotus of the lady's face to close. But if Tushára be taken as a proper name, Vishnu becomes an epithet following the tone.

"The lotus face is compared to Lakshmi (glory).

"In the 4th line, the word *Satvato* means a follower of Vishnu.

"The word *Matanaprado* is doubtful. I have rendered it as an epithet. If it be taken as a proper name, the grammar becomes faulty, as in line 2nd; for it then could not coalesce into one word with the epithet which follows. It would require a *syo*, the mark of the genitive case, as in the epithet which precedes it.

"When I submitted this inscription to the learned translator, I brought to his notice the name or epithet *Tushára*, which occurs in the 2nd line in connection with the purely Hindû name of Vishnu. In my account of the Mathura inscriptions, in which the name of the Tushâra king Vasu Deva occurs so often, I pointedly drew attention to this evidence of the early adoption of Hindû names by the Indo-Scythians. I then suggested the identity of this Vasu Deva of the coins and inscriptions with Vasu Deva the first of the four princes of the Kanwa dynasty, according to the lists of the Puranas.

"I now propose to identify the present Tushâra chief Vishnu with the 3rd Kanwa prince named Narayana, who reigned from A.D. 57 to 69. This identification is corroborated by the date of Ghatotkacha, who, as the father of Chandra Gûpta I., must have reigned from about A.D. 50 to 79, so that he and the Kanwa prince Narayana were actually contemporaries. According to my view, the Kanwas (or Tushâras of India) held sway in Mathura, Delhi, and the Panjâb until A.D. 79, when their power was either subverted altogether, or much reduced in extent by Chandra Gûpta I., to whom the consolidation of the Gûpta dominions was certainly due, as he is the first of the race who assumed the title of king of kings, or Mâharâjâdhirâja.

"The name of Tushâm itself also appears to me to be derived from these Tushâra princes, as its original form was most probably *Tushârarâma*, or the 'Tushâra Monastery,'[1] which was first shortened to Tushârâm, and then to Tushâm. I conclude, therefore, that the neighbouring fortress of Hânsî, which in later times became the headquarters of the first Musalmân king, Kutb-ûd-dîn, have been one of the chief strongholds of the Indo-Scythian princes in Northern India."

HISSAR.

I made a very short stay at Hissar, as the place has been previously examined, and described in the Archæological Survey Reports, Vol. V, pp. 140-142.

Crowning a low isolated rock a little to the north of that of Toshâm, I found a mediæval castle which is said to have been erected by the celebrated Chohân emperor Prithvi-Râj, as a kacheri or law-court, and hence it is called *Prithvi-Râj ka Kacheri* by the Hindî-speaking people, and by the more Persianised folk simply *Bâradarî*—a modernism no doubt derived from the number of entrances the building displays exteriorly, *i.e.*, twelve, though in reality it possesses sixteen openings. *Prithvi-Râj's Kachêri* is built of dressed stone and lime, upon two successive platforms, constructed of the same material. The highest of these platforms rises above the lower 7′, and measures 41′ from north to south, and 37′ 4″ from east to west, while the lower *farash* or floor measures 97′ north and south, and 61′ 5″ east and west.

[1] I could find no monastery in the neighbourhood. But a portion of the ruins surmounting the inscribed hill, which are generally regarded as the remains of a fort, may represent such a monastery.—H. B. W. G.

The plan of the castle is a cross, each wing being 15′ high and projecting 11′ from the main central building, which is covered in by a dome, the summit of which is 30′ above the floor of the hall and 16′ in diameter.

The sixteen openings before mentioned are without gates or doors, and measure 6½′ high; four of these are in the central hall and therefore unseen from without, hence "twelve-gated," the modern name of this edifice. (See Plate IX.)

The picturesque hill town of Toshâm is immediately managed by a *thânadâr* and six *lambardârs*, two of whom are Musalmâns and four Hindûs; these numbers also give the approximate proportion of the abstract castes of the population, apparently an honest and industrious one, the agricultural section contriving to raise crops from sand hillocks in a truly marvellous manner, while the *banyas* or merchants and bankers show their public spirit by constructing handsome rest-houses for travellers and pilgrims to *Bân Ganga.* Good examples of these rest-houses may be seen in many parts of this neighbourhood, *e.g.*, at the *Kadwârâtâl* near Toshâm.

I cannot close this account of Toshâm without gratefully acknowledging the assistance and information rendered to me by the Jaina priest in charge of the modern shrine on the Toshâm-pahâr, called Paras Nâth ka Math. This good man has resided here long, and has assumed the name of his titular divinity.

8.—LOHÂRÛ.

This town is situated 36 miles to the south of Tosham and on the road to Jaypur. In the fort of Lohârû, which is said to be 150 years old, there is a large mosque and the Nawâb's private dwelling. But the fort itself—a modern six-towered structure—possesses little to interest the archæologist.

Apparently the oldest building at Lohârû is a large *Sûrya* temple, situated just outside the fort and called *Sekar-band;* and there are two smaller Hindû shrines inside the town, which contain idols belonging to the Vaishnava sect.

But the buildings best seen from a distance, and which lend dignity to the exterior appearance of Lohârû, are the mosques ; that near the bazâr being built only 19 years ago by a certain Captain Wazir Muhammad Beg. There are about 350 houses proper to this *qasbeh*, besides a number of straggling dwellings and cenotaphs (*chhatre*) outside.

In Lord Lake's time, Ahmad Bakhsh Khân, the progenitor of the present Nawâbs of Lohârû, ruled at Ferozepore close by, and it is said that Lohârû was then made over to him for military services rendered to the British Government. Before this, however, the place belonged to, and was ruled by, independent Thâkûrs, and was, according to local tradition, the scene of constant feuds and pitched battles. These quarrels culminated in the invasion, in V.S. 1828=A.D. 1772, of Râjâ Bhopâl Singh, who, though assisted by numerous Râis of Singhana, Khetrî, &c., was repulsed with severe loss by the Thâkûrs of Lohârû, who ultimately slew him and twenty-seven of his nobles, and buried them in *chabûtras* which are still pointed out, the Râjâ Bhopâl Singh being interred in the large *chabûtra*, or "square mound," outside the town.

A common-looking grave here is much esteemed and even worshipped by the people (especially Hindûs) of Lohârû. This *chabûtra* is said to contain the remains of a dog, formerly possessed by the chief of the victorious Thâkûrs, which is credited with having been foremost in, and borne the brunt of, the Khetrî-Lohârû battle, and springing up and seizing the invading warriors' throats, it is said this dog thus slew a large number of the enemy ; but in the end being itself slain, it was buried on this spot with beat of drum, and has since been an object of worship and homage. Were it not for the *sagparast* of Naishapûr, mentioned in Khûsrû's charming darvish tales, this example of dog-worship would probably be unique.

9.—NARNAUL.

Narnaul is 32 miles due west of Bawal, a station on the railway between Hissar and Jaypur. It is stated that the city of Narnaul was at first founded under the Dhosîhils, and was ruled by the *Jogîs*, or devotees, who enjoyed a high repute for their spiritual attainments. The date of the foundation of this city is said to be in the word *Narnaul*, and may be ascertained by the mode of computation called *Abjad*.

The derivation of the name of this city is related in three ways:—

1st.—Its name was *Nahar Naul*,—*i.e.*, "the forest of tigers," because numerous tigers were to be found there.

2nd.—Its name was *Nar Naul*, *nar* meaning "woman" in the local *patois*, and *naul* "beautiful," because it is said that it contained beautiful women.

3rd.—Its name was *Nâg Naul*,—*i.e.*, when the city was founded, a mongoose was seen fighting with a serpent; hence the name from *nâga*, "a snake," and *newal*, "a mongoose."

It is related that subsequently Hazrat Turkaman came to India with jewels in one hand and a sword in the other, and fought several bloody battles with the Rathors at Narnaul. Hazrat Turkaman was killed in A.H. 531, 1137 A.D.[1]

The principal buildings, &c., here are as follows:—

1st.—The school (*madrasa*) is one of the greatest buildings in the city. In the above-mentioned building is the tomb of Hasan Sîve, great-grandfather of Shêr Shâh. This tomb was built by Shêr Shâh at an expense, I was assured, of about a lakh of rupees. Its date on an inscription tells us that it was erected in 927 A.H. by Shêr Shâh, resident of a village called Simla; at present the village belongs to the Râja of Khetrî.

[1] Narnaul has ever been famous for its *Mendî* or *Mendhî* henna, which is a red dye for the tips of the fingers: women often affect this habit of reddening their fingers. Hence the couplet which I can now remember as having seen somewhere, though, as I quote from memory, perhaps write inaccurately:—

Mendhi biâr az Narnaul Jorî biâr az Gûzrât. "Bring Mendhi from Narnaul; bring a pair (? of shoes) from Gûzrât."

2nd.—The tank and the house of Khân Sarwar, which were excavated and built respectively at a large cost, and near it is the lake of Khalil Sarwar. The last two buildings were erected by Nawâb Shâh and Quli Khân, Mahram Bahartoe. The Nawâb was the governor of Narnaul in the time of Jalâl-ûd-dîn Akbar for fifty-two years. A handsome tomb was built by Nawâb Shâh Quli Khân in 986 A.H. This was erected by the Khân in his lifetime for his father. Another building, named *Tripoliah*, or "the three-gated," was erected by the same Nawâb in 997 A.H. at a large expense; and a Jamâ Masjîd in the old fort was built in 999 A.H. He also built a river bridge which still exists. Besides these, many of the buildings erected by the Nawâb are now in ruins, but the foundations of many of them still exists, as in the examples already mentioned. A building named Chattar was erected by Lâlâ Râi Mukand Sâhib, Mansabdâr, in Shâh Jahân's time. He also built a sarai in which now the court of the Nizâmat of the Mahârâja of Patiâlâ is held. The tomb of Hazarat Shâh, Nizâm at Narnaul, was built in the time of Shâh Jálâl-ud-dîn Akbar. It contains a grand mosque erected by Nûr-ud-dîn Jahângir, and hence is called the Great Hazîra. On the north side, between the city and the village of Dharson, is a building named Chor Gaud, built by Jamâl Khân, an Afghân.

I shall conclude this account of the objects at Narnaul by mentioning a Baoli which was built in the time of the Emperor Akbar by a person named Ali Khân; and another building, containing 9 square courtyards and having a great deal of marble-work, was erected by Dewân Harkant Râi.

The visitor to Narnaul is impressed on entering the city by the large proportion which the ruined buildings bear to those in use; whole streets appear to be tumbling down and fast decaying.

10.—VAIRÂDA, BAIRÂT (VAIRÂTA OR BHÎM-GÂM).

The town of Bairât is situated in the midst of a valley in the immediate neighbourhood of Jaypur. The population of the *qasbeh*, or town, of Bairát is now 1,500 souls, of which number two thirds are Hindûs. But the town, which is protected by a moat, contains little of interest besides the fort, which is comparatively modern, small, and much out of repair. The original historical town of the Pandûs was more to the east of the valley, where there is still a ruined site called *Bhîmjî-ka-gâm*, or "Bhîm's village," which is said to be situated on the site of the ancient city.

It may be of service to future visitors to Bairât here to correct a misnomer,—I allude to the name by which a prominent object in this valley has been called in previous accounts,—*i.e.*, "The Pandû's Hill." This hill is invariably called by people and guides, "Bhîm's Hill" (*Bhîmjî-kâ-dongar*) or "Bhîm's Cave" (*Bhîmjî-kâ-Gophâ*), and never "The Pandû's Hill." Though this difference is small (merely the substitution of the family patronymic for the proper name of one of its members), it is eminently calculated to confuse travellers;[1] it certainly lost some time for me in enquiring for the particular hill.

With so much that is excellent already written about Bairât it will be difficult to add to our information concerning this beautiful, and perhaps unique, old vale, unless we draw a little on the mythological or classical account preserved by Parohîts, Brâhmans, and others. One needs to draw sparingly on such an account, should one's reputation for sanity be desirable, and so I confine myself to one single selection which seeks to account for the origin, or rather the migration, of Bhîm's Hill. It is said, then, that this rugged pile of boulders is the offspring of *Girrâj* or *Govardhan*, the celebrated mountain near Brindraban and Mathûra, which places formed the little world of the pastoral hero or incarnate deity Krishna, who is believed to have saved his homestead from the fury of Indra

[1] Some of whom may search in vain for a "Yellow" *Pandû* hill if the five celebrated brothers happen to be out of mind.

by holding the mountain suspended in mid-air (*vide* Bhagvat Pûrân, Book X), and that Bhîmjî separated and carried it from the parent mountain to Bhairât, where he bored the caves we now see, as a *sirna*, or sanctuary, for the fraternity to dwell in during the last year of their long banishment by the Kuru section of the family. A hollow near the summit is pointed out as that formed by Bhîm's foot. The cavity did not appear to me to resemble, in the smallest degree, a foot-print, but this it would seem is a mere matter of opinion, as the Brâhmans then present considered it a correct impression of the *bhîma-pada*.

On the top of *Bhîmji dongar* and near this supposed foot-print, are some Bairâgîs' or hermits' dwellings, and here an annual *mêlâ*, or fair, takes place on the light fortnight, 2nd of August, according to the lunar year of the Hindûs, or, as they express it, *Miti Bhadon-doj-sûdi*, which is the anniversary of the day on which Bhîm's Hill was miraculously transported from Govardhan to Vairâda.

Of the ruins east of the present town, already mentioned as Bhîm's village, it will be well to give some further account, as these are undoubtedly the remains of the ancient city renowned in Hindû history as the sanctuary of the Five Pandû Brothers during a portion of their exile.

In the first place, the name above given (*i.e.*, *Bhîm gâm*) is merely the vulgar one of this spot, whose correct name, known only to a few of the more intelligent Gaur Brâhmans of the neighbourhood, is Vairâda with the cerebral *ḍ*, thus: वैराड़ : I feel sure in this word we have the original form of this famous village's name.

These remains are situated, as nearly as I could estimate, about half a mile due east of the present town, and consist mostly of conglomerate boulder ruins resting on the inner mountain chain which encircles the valley. The space between these remains and the comparatively modern *qasbeh* is evenly strewn with broken brick and pottery all the way, and as these traces of antiquity and former occupation extend for a few hundred yards west of the *qasbeh*, I would assign an area of somewhat less than three fourths of a mile for the ancient city east and west. These traces are not clearly visible north and south, but probably the extent this way was about the same as the *veds* or educated Brâhmans speak of the *Chokas-pûra Pandû-kâ*, or the "Rectangular (square?) City of Pandûs."

I gathered from local sources that the inscription, which formerly lent its name to the *Bijak Pahâr* near the south-west pass, was cut out from this rock bodily by an European in V.S. 1891. It occurred to me that this European might have been Lieutenant-Colonel Tod, who deprived this country of many of its inscriptions, *e.g.*, that of Hânsî.

There is a massive stone *band*, or reservoir (now quite broken), and several *sati* monuments and cenotaphs, some rather handsome, to the north-east of the Bhim's Hill.

11.—AMBA OR AMBIR.

Leaving Bairât for Jaipur, &c., and proceeding south a little west, a comparatively easy mountain pass is encountered, crossed, and the Amlodia hills, stretching away in the direction of Ghatwâra, present a more extensive view than those of the valley of Vairâda.

The scenery in this locality is rendered beautifully picturesque by the countless palm groves which increase gradually but steadily in numbers and luxuriance with every mile traversed from the Amlodia range to Kot Pûtli and thence to Jaipur; indeed, the different, and decidedly improving, character of the scenery is marked after leaving the Panjâb to the north, and this is perhaps more fully appreciated by the traveller who has just toiled through that province, particularly ugly from Lahor to its southern extremity; and he is thankful to exchange the arid, comfortless country of the five rivers, with its dirty ill-stocked Sikh villages, brackish water, and sandy roads, for such scenery as is found in the well-wooded hilly district of Râjwâra, numerously studded with boulder-built towns and villages, now resting in some shady valley, now picturesquely running up the side of yonder rocky hill which probably supplied the material for the construction of the village it bears.

Ghatwâra possesses a small hill fortress perched on a minor brow of the Amlodia mountain system near which the village of Ghatwâra is built. The fort belongs to the Thâkûr of Chamû, and is said to be old. As it is merely representative of the kind of strongholds abounding here, I did not spend any time in examining the Ghatwâra fort, than which that of Achror 20 miles north of Jaipur is perhaps a better example.

En route from Bairât to Jaipur and about midway between these places, I noticed a very small village, which, however, possesses a fine temple (apparently Jain), four sculptured and inscribed *Sâtî Maths*, and, what is of infinitely more importance, the place is called *Bûddhasthân*, and I found a *bas-relief* of the *Bûddha-pada* with the lotus, &c. This sculpture is called *Bishan-pad*, or Vishnû's feet. But I suspect from the appearance of the temple, and the still preserved name of this village, that Bûddhasthân is an ancient site where there may have formerly existed Buddhistic establishments among these rocks; the hamlet only contains about 25 souls at present.

In passing over the ruins of Amba, one is forcibly reminded of the Eternal City; for at Amba commerce and even the arts appear to thrive amidst desolation. Indeed, the deserted capital of Dhundâr may well be likened to a diminutive Rome. Idols, columns, bases, capitals, and richly-sculptured friezes lay strewn about in picturesque confusion from the foot to brow of the neighbouring hills, and inside the town itself these relics, once portions of temples and idol-shrines, form seats and door-steps for the *Kachhwahan* traders and artizans.

Passing under the brow of fortified hills, one enters Ambir from the north through massive portals, the gates of which are covered with plates of iron and decorated by embossed metal panels. Further on, an infinity of ruins are passed ere the inhabited portion of the town is reached. Let it not, however, be imagined that these ruins are altogether tenantless, for, inhospitable as they appear—doorless, windowless, roofless, and, in many instances, without walls—nooks and corners are found by the lower classes and converted into

The town proper once reached, the crowd thickens and approaches the density of cities; here, too, are some fine old buildings intact, the most noteworthy being a Saivite temple of stone, magnificently sculptured in every part, "from parapet to basement." This shrine is situated in close proximity to the Darogah's house, itself remarkable for its elaborately stuccoed pagoda-like façade, which is neatly decorated in fresco; but this, with many other buildings, of course belong to a much later date than the first-mentioned stone temple. Further still to the south, we pass out of the present town, when, excepting the handsome palace, tank, and repaired fortifications, all is again ruin, until the well-constructed road leading over the hills into Jaipur is approached.

Having started from Achror with the intention of marching into Jaipur, whither my forward tents had preceded me, I did not stay long at Amba, and in these few notes taken *en passant* much has doubtless escaped my observation. I, however, rambled for a few hours over these extensive remains and regretted my inability to examine them more minutely. Amba is described in Vol. II, p. 250, of the Archæological Survey Reports.

12.—JAIPUR.

I made a very short stay at the modern Jaipur, which city is uninteresting archæologically, and, in the rigid angularity of its plan, excessively ugly. The roads are pretentiously paved along the centre with slabs of stone, and this is very bad for carriages. Matters are not by any means improved by the universal coat of pink-colour wash (often rendered more hideous and paltry by floral ornamentations in whitewash) which the buildings *en masse* appear to have received. Everything *inside* this city, then, smacks of brandnewness, bad taste, and a hankering after European characteristics.

Extramurally we are no better off, for there is little of interest to see; therefore, after putting in train the arrangements for my intended visit to Ranthambhaur, a fortress in this State of Jaipur (as special State permission is necessary ere this fort can be examined), I started for Ajmêr.

13.—AJMÊR.

The etymology of this name has already been fully discussed. *Ajmêr* is most probably derived from *Aja*, "a goat," and *mêrû*, according to Hindû theology, a sacred mountain in the Himalayas; but *mêrû* has since been contracted into simply *mêr*, and applied indiscriminately to *any* hill, mountain, or range of mountains. The city of Ajmêr is sufficiently close to the great Aravali range to have acquired the suffix, common enough in such cases, of *mêr;* and the long, narrow strip of land forming the district of *Mêrwâra* probably owes its name also to these mountains,—*i.e.*, "the neighbourhood" (*wâra*) of "mountains" (*mêra*).

Mêr has obviously the same significance as *nêr*, often similarly applied to other place names (the nasal following easier certain consonants than the labial in certain spoken dialects),—*e.g.*, *Bhatnêr* is much easier pronounced than would be Bhatmêr.

To the nomadic origin of Ajmêr, too, its name affords a ready clue.

As a field for archæological exploration, Ajmêr has been "oft ploughed and well ploughed," and though it could not complain of neglect in this respect were it suffered to lay fallow awhile, I have availed myself of the opportunity afforded to me during a short sojourn here to add my humble quota of information to the already ample stock accessible on the subject.

It is well known that, as far back as the reign of James I., Ajmêr afforded matter for European annotation and comment, and thus in the Journal of Sir Thomas Roe, the famous envoy from the court of that monarch to the Great Mughal, Jehângir, we have several most interesting, if somewhat quaint, descriptions, and valuable topographical details. At a much later period Colonel Tod examined the place to excellent purpose.[1]

[1] Tod's Western India.

Later still the architectural remains were critically examined and reported on by General Cunningham.[1]

The authorities have sanctioned a certain sum of money which has been expended on a partial restoration of the large mosque known as the *Arhai-din-ke-Jhopri.* Works of this nature cannot be conducted with too much care, and it is a want of this care that has rendered the very word "restoration," as applied to many buildings in India, equal to "demolition." These restorations, then, have not been happy.[2]

In support of my view, I will content myself with a few notes on the most glaring errors of commission and omission.

The repairs of the *relievo* inscriptions and ornamentation on the façade seem to have been regarded as of more importance than the completion of the broken-off *minârs* crowning the building proper; the *minâr* towers of the cloisters, which are daily becoming lower, appear to have been totally ignored.

The original work on the façade is of a pleasing buff colour:[3] the repairs have been carried forward with white lime! thus covering the somewhat imposing frontage with white spots, as though it had just weathered a heavy snow-storm. These mortar-patches, which might have been left for the last work, if they were necessary at all, are rough and uneven, nor can the façade of this building be "restored" back again to the condition in which the modern architect found it; for the lime has far too firm a hold on the time-honoured work it defaces to allow of any such benevolent scheme being put in practice now.

The roof of the *Arhai-din-ke-Jhopri* has been covered with a most astonishing and heterogeneous collection of temple *sikris* or *kalas,—i.e.*, the cogg-wheel-shaped ornaments which surmount the *sikris*, or "steeples," of Hindû temples; these appear to have been planted about wherever

[1] Archæological Reports, Vol. II, pp. 252—263.

[2] In 1875-76 the Government sanctioned R14,000 for these restorations.

[3] Being executed in a compact and close-grained, light-yellow stone.

caprice dictated, and assuredly do not improve the appearance of this ill-used building.

One of the minor architraves (that near the centre arch) is quite 8″ out of its true horizontal position, but I could not learn whether this too is a part of the restorations; most probably it is. The south-end cupola is at present lying in many fragments in the courtyard of this mosque, while the ceiling from which it fell admits freely the sun's rays, being open in the centre to the sky.

But the most lamentable instance of unappreciative neglect is the condition of the outer cloisters of this mosque in the centre. These cloisters, together with their originally tall minarets, furnish a monument of Musalmân architectural adaptation that should by every possible means be preserved and rendered permanent. Unhappily time and ages of neglect combined have brushed away more than two thirds of the graceful minaret on the north-east, and quite half of its fellow on the south-east corner of the cloisters; and these minarets, when I last visited Ajmêr and measured them from the road, stood 24′ 1″ and 34′ 7″ high respectively, being 14′ 9″ in girth at their bases. The exquisitely-designed fluting and ornamental bands still extant, of these columns, may be seen in Plate X, where I have endeavoured to preserve a record of all that remains of the least broken *minâr*.

The cloisters have fared even worse than their minarets. Here the only bit of original work exists on the south side of the courtyard, and comprises, in all, 164′ of these buildings, in three disjointed pieces; and as the total length of the courtyard this way (east and west) is 264′ 6″, the portion uncovered by cloisters now missing is 100′ 6″, thus:—

Commencing from the west end.

1st part	83′	of ancient	cloistered	walling.
3rd ,,	26′	,,	,,	,,
5th ,,	55′	,,	,,	,,
Total .	164′			

2nd part 31′ 3″ of bare space.
4th ,, 21′ ,, ,, ,,
6th ,, 48′ 3″ ,, ,, ,,

Total . 100′ 6″

Although some hideous barrack-like sheds have been constructed to the east of the courtyard, absolutely nothing has been done to *repair* the last fragments that remain of a richly-cloistered courtyard which would hold its own with that of the Kuṭb Masjid at Delhi.

I observed some new buildings still in embryo, and evidently intended for new versions of the old cloisters to the north-west corner of the quadrangle. But these are smaller and even more ill-formed than the eastern sheds before alluded to. Little of these cloisters remains to guide us, it is true, but if taken in time this little would suffice for their effective restoration—I should say, re-building; for before we can restore to the great mosque at Ajmêr its cloisters, almost three angles of the entire quadrangle must be rebuilt, for, as already shewn, only 164′ is left of their original extent of 770′, allowing a deduction for the entrance to the east and the space proper to the mosque on the west. So far, however, from any action being taken for their conservation, the well-dressed stones, of which the old cloisters are built, daily become fewer, and for this fact I can personally vouch, as I lately visited the cloistered walling thrice, and, between my first and last visit, distinctly marked the disappearance of at least four large dressed stones which projected like irregular teeth from three broken and rugged edges of the only existing (south) piece of this precious relic. A like process of unchecked peculation has already cleared away three fourths of this old cloistered monastery, leaving not the vestige of a trace to mark its former course, and, if permitted to continue, it is no difficult matter to predict that what is left to us will shortly be exhausted to provide building materials for the rapidly growing city of Ajmêr. In short, these cloisters, which formed the most extensive part of the Ajmêr mosque, and which are covered with masons' marks of very early date and specially interesting to the archæologist on that account, are regarded as a lawful quarry whence finely-dressed stones of all dimensions can be removed and appropriated *ad libitum!*

I secured a photograph of all that remains of the cloisters from the south-west angle to the centre of the south side of the courtyard (exactly 132′), and, by repeating this, a true idea of their present state may be gleaned, though the piece still standing to the east of the large domed building is only from 3′ to 4′ in height, so that in the photograph which I have prepared for future use (scale 6′ to 1″) we have virtually *all* that exists.

The first piece of cloistering stands at present 21′ above the courtyard floor inside, and 40′ above the road-level outside; the third piece, measured similarly inside and outside, is 15′ and 35′ high respectively. These dimensions are commenced from the western, or mosque, end of the courtyard, and, I need scarcely say, are the mean of several measurements taken.

The thickness of the solid portions of these cloisters is 6′; that of the monastic dwellings may be judged from the elevations, as they are invariably square, and hence their depth north and south is the same as their width west and east shown in the elevation.

From the *Arhai-din-ke-Jhopri* to the old fortress of Târagarh the road leads through a portion of Indragarh, which is the oldest locality here, and is said to have been the site of the first city.

Here we have the tomb of the celebrated Muhammadan saint, Hazrat Khwâja Múen-ûd-dîn Chushti, with all its surroundings,—*e.g.*, metal caldrons for preparing the feasts in, &c.[1] This tomb it is that lends to the place whatever sanctity it may have in the eyes of Muhammadans, and the entombed Khwâja has retained his popularity to the present day in a most remarkable manner. That he was formerly popular, and that attention to his *manes* was fashionable in

1 See the account anent this festive ceremony in the Râjpûtâna Gazetteer.

the early Mughal days, is evidenced by the fact that both Hûmâyûn and his illustrious son Akbar were amongst the distinguished pilgrims who visited this tomb. The Persianised name of the place, much affected by Musalmâns,—*i.e.*, *Ajmêr Sharîf*, or "the holy Ajmêr,"—also owes its existence entirely to this much-venerated sepulchre.

The ascent to the fort is gradual, and an excellent road for pedestrians is provided the whole way, and, long before reaching the fort, several isolated tombs and minor shrines may be seen from the road. The tombs, I understand, are, for the most part, those of the unlucky Muhammadan invaders who were doomed never to see the fort their comrades ultimately took, but to die by defensive Râjpût arms on the way.

I spent two days on Târagarh, or "the star citadel," and that barely sufficed to enable me to supplement the existing accounts of the celebrated fortress with the following scraps of information.

Is it among things generally known that Târagarh possesses exactly 9 portals, 4 major and 5 minor ones, each having a local name proper to itself? If it is, I think the *exact* number of bastions surrounding this fortress (*i.e.*, 16) with their positions according to the local designation of each (for even these have separate names) is not.

On first hearing the name *Âr-pâr-ke-aṭṭa* hurriedly pronounced, I thought that it may have been derived from that of *Appa* or *Jai-appa*, the famous Maharatta general, whose visits to Ajmêr must have been rather frequent. But on further enquiry I found that the name, in the spoken *bhâkha*, signifies the bastion commanding both "this and that side" of the mountain ravines. Again, *Hakâni-Bakâni Sayed Ṣâḥab-ka-bûrj* may possibly be a mere corruption of *Akhwân Saiyed-Ṣâḥabân-ke-bûrj*,[1] or "the bastion of the Saiyed brothers," who virtually ruled India on the decline of the Mughal authority, and whom Tod calls, in his shrewd way, "the Warwicks of India."[2]

[1] More correctly *Burj-i-Ikhwan* Sayyed *Sâhabân*.

[2] Tod's Râjasthân.

On the road to Târagarh, the city of Ajmêr is passed through, after which the mosque of *Arhai-din-ke-Jhopri* and Indragarh can be taken *en route* to the fort. After ascending the admirable winding road for a considerable distance the *Lakshmīpol*, or "gate of wealth" (one of the few old Hindû names left), is reached; the second gate is much broken, its roof having fallen in, and hence it is known far and wide as the *Phûṭe-darwâzah*, or the "broken gate;" the third gateway (exterior) is called *Gûgûdi-ki-phâṭak;* the fourth, *Ghângat* (or *Ghûngas*)-*ke-darwâzah;* and the fifth, *Futteḥ-darwâzah*, or "the gate of victory," in gaining which so many brave warriors have perished.

The victory gate is the principal entrance to Târagarh, and, with the exception of a small postern (*khirki*) which leads *through the centre* of the fourth bastion (counting eastwards from the *Futteḥ-darwâzah*), is the only one used. It can very easily be rendered inaccessible.

The remaining portals are to the north-west, and serve to guard the road from the plains across the first and lowest, to the second semi-circular road on the range above, which continues its southerly course as far as the fortifications thrown across the northern edge of a deep ravine on the west side of Târagarh.

The first-named gateway—*i.e.*, that nearest the plains—is called *Bhâvani-pol*, "goddess' gate," another of the old names so rare here; the second, *Hatia-pol*, "elephant's gate;" and the third, *Ar-kot-ke-darwâzah*, or "the gateway of the covered fortifications," beyond which is a deep valley now partially cultivated.

Counting eastwards from the principal gateway, which is the *Fatteḥ-darwâzah*, the first three bastions take their names from the exterior portals already mentioned, *viz.*, *Ghûngat* or *Ghûngas-ke-darwâzah*, from which its approximate bastion is called *Ghûngat* or *Ghûngas-ke-bûrj; Gûgadi-ke-phâtak*, from which its approximate bastion is called *Gûgadi-ke-bûrj;* and *Phûta-darwâzah*, from which its neighbouring bastion takes the name of *Phûta-bûrj*. But all the remaining bastions have separate names. The fourth bastion on this side (that called *Bâla-kill'ah-bûrj*) is situate close to what I understand to be a clergyman's residence, as it is called "*Pâdri Sâhab-ka-bangaleh;*" the fifth, or *Singâr-Chaûri-bûrj*, near the Deputy Commissioner's house; the sixth, *Âr-pâr-ke-aṭṭa*, and the seventh (*Janû-naik-ke-bûrj*), are near the railway buildings; the eighth bastion, called *Pipli-wâlla-bûrj*, is situated near the tank called *Bara-jhâla;* the ninth, or *Baharâni Shahid-Sâhab-ka-bûrj*, is near the celebrated tomb of this martyr and also in close proximity to another Musalmân's *dargâh;* the tenth bastion of the main or inner wall, called *Daura-bûrj*, is almost *on* the track which leads to the Nasîrâbâd road; the eleventh (also of the main circumvallation), called *Bandra-bûrj*, is flanked on the north-west by a deep ravine and on the south-east by a large *kûnd* or "tank;" the twelfth bastion, called *Imli-wâlla-bûrj*, is near the palace of *Rûtha Râni*, or "the angry queen," and also near the pleasure garden of the Emperor Jahângir, called *Nûr-cheshmeh*, or "the fountain of light;" the thirteenth bastion takes its name (*Futteh-bûrj*) from the adjacent and principal gate of the citadel.

It only remains to mention the three bastions on the fortified promontory which juts out of the main fortress to the west, and we shall have the situations of all the gates and bastions of Târagarh fixed by their local bearings. The bastion standing on the extremity of this promontory (and which we may call the fourteenth of Târagarh, though it is really the first of these outworks) is called *Hûsên-bûrj*, and overlooks the deep ravine through which runs a road leading to Nasîrâbâd; the fifteenth bastion, or that called *Hakâni-bakâni-Saiyed-Sâhab-ka-bûrj*, overlooks a line of rugged rocks amongst which are two *kûnds* or water reservoirs; while the sixteenth and concluding bastion, called *Imli-wâlla-bûrj*, is partly overshadowed by an old tamarind tree (*Tamarindus indica*) from which it takes its name.

I obtained these names from an old Musalmân who was born on Târagarh, and has continued to live there since his birth. Indeed, he is apparently the only man who knows all these names, having professedly made it a point to remember them. Several natives in the hamlet near the *Futteh-bûrj* can recollect a few of the more prominent of these old names, but wholly fail with regard to some of the more obscure gates and *all* the bastions to the south, which are perhaps the most interesting. There can be little doubt, then, that my old informant, who belongs more to the past than present generation, is favoured with an exceptional memory, and that, when he shall have passed away, he will carry many of these names with him.

It would hardly be credited from its meagre appearance that the small village on Târagarh contains 80 dwellings and 500 inhabitants; yet such are the numbers with which my enquiries on the subject were answered.

Before closing these notes on Ajmêr, I will mention a highly interesting discovery which is due to the able investigations made by Mr. Sandford of the Railway Department here. I allude to a pillared stone chamber which, from its generally massive construction and the heavy—disproportionately heavy—capitals of its supporting columns, must belong to the Hindû period, and, therefore, is unique, for with the exception of this single building I do not know of any Hindû structure on Târagarh. The small, modern village temples, or such buildings as have been constructed from the spoils of Hindû buildings by Muhammadan agency, are, of course, not taken into consideration.

A similar Hindû building exists inside the fortifications now called "the Magazine" near the city of Ajmêr, and in both these rare examples the capitals bear a strong resemblance in outline to each other and remind one of the Persepolitan capitals. I have said that the resemblance rests in the *outline*, and here it ceases, as no animals have been represented. But the bare proportions are sufficiently striking to warrant the comparison, and these capitals appear as though the sculptor had blocked them out as a preliminary step before embellishing them with dual figures of lions, centaurs, or bulls on either side.

The ancient stone chamber on Târagarh is situated behind, or to the west of, a range of barracks, and therefore remains quite concealed until the barracks are entered and passed through, when it is exposed. The floor of this chamber, which is of stone slabs, is found to be considerably below the level of the present barrack buildings. Stepping down to the floor, the chamber is found to be a flat-roofed, cell-like apartment containing 30 pillars of stone, each 11 feet high, which gives us also the height of this chamber interiorly; the exterior height being 14 feet 1 inch, and by a comparison of these two dimensions we may conclude the stone roof to be 3 feet 1 inch in thickness. The interior length (north and south) of this room is 46 feet 3 inches, and its breadth interiorly 20 feet 3 inches. Measured from outside, these dimensions become 50 feet 2½ inches and 24 feet 2½ inches for length and breadth respectively, so that the thickness of wall throughout must be 1 foot 11¾ inches.

There were formerly 32 pillars in this ancient stone chamber, but 2 of these have been extracted of late years for some purpose of utility connected with the soldiers' accommodation.[1] For a similar reason, I understand, three openings or skylights have been made in the flat roof above the last or western row of columns, and these must have been sorely needed, for, even with their aid, the chamber is poorly lighted and ventilated. The pillars in this chamber are arranged in four rows running longitudinally, and having originally 8 pillars to each row. But of these 32 pillars, 2 have been extracted from the second row, as one passes by the eastern doorway through the barracks. These pillars are squares of 1 foot side or 4 feet in circuit, for 3 feet above the floor-level (from which 10 inches must be deducted for their angular bases), above which they are octagons of 3 feet 7 inches circuit for a space of 5 feet, and the remaining 3 feet of the above-named height of 11 feet is made up by their massive capital. There are here three doorways and seven window openings, each 7 feet and 4 feet high respectively, and distributed over the chamber as follows :—

(1) Doorway in the centre of each of the sides, and
(2) windows at each end of the east, west, and south

[1] The chamber is now a part of the modern barracks to which the invalid soldiers resort during the warm months, on account of the elevation and other sanitary advantages of Târagarh.

faces; the north face having only one small window opened in the centre.

In front of the barracks which run along the eastern face of this early stone chamber, I observed a few broken sculptures, and, according to a local tradition, there were formerly 3 tanks or reservoirs here—1 for water, 1 for clarified butter (*ghee*), and 1 for oil; and these tanks are said to have stood the several former possessors of Târagarh in good stead when they were besieged and denied egress and ingress from and to the fort in quest of supplies. But the place has all been filled up now and forms a level courtyard betwixt the barrack lines.

Nobody seems to know for what purpose this chamber was used by its builders, though a general belief exists on Târagarh that it was a *kachèri* or *dewân* (civil law court); and this is quite probable, for one cannot well imagine its construction for a dwelling, as it must have been very dark, comfortless, and cold in the days of *Vaisaldeva;* and, though any alterations to such archæological relics is generally to be deprecated, I confess the skylights lately made in the roof and before mentioned are a decided improvement. Taking all into consideration, I venture to think that this chamber was originally designed for a public building of some kind, either a law court, assembly room, or hospital.

The construction of the walls of Târagarh reminded me much of that employed in the trans-Indus country. In both cases the wall is necessarily very massive, consumes more material, and occupies more space than it would were a better class of masonry resorted to. The principle on which these walls are erected seems to be a very slovenly one, and the exterior appearance is decidedly irregular and unworkmanlike; while the durability and strength are alike impaired. Each wall is in reality two walls, each generally about 18 inches thick, built with mortar and boulders, some of which are partially dressed and others wholly undressed, for I have observed both descriptions used indiscriminately. These outer walls stand apart, leaving an aperture between, which varies according to the thickness finally required. When these two outer shell-like walls are ready, the space between is forthwith filled up by stones of all shapes and sizes, tumbled in pell-mell from above, often without any mortar preparation whatsoever; shales, or wedges of stone, are then inserted from without wherever a gap or interstice is seen. In the fortress of Ajmêr, however, I noticed a favourable, though but partial, departure from this method, and here the circumvallation is commenced almost invariably on a sandstone basis, formed of carefully squared and dressed blocks of sandstone, which often attains nearly one fifth of the wall's entire height, but the line is irregular horizontally, being in some places higher, in others lower, and in too many places the sandstone blocks are omitted altogether. It occurred to me at one time that these blocks are all that remain of the earliest or original fortifications; and that the superstructure belongs to a later period; but this theory is hardly tenable, and it would be somewhat hypercritical at this time of day to burden Târagarh with any more periods. It is possible that the first and original fort was entirely built of such sandstone blocks as now form the basis of its circumvallation, but, seeing that the rubble-work is undoubtedly of Hindû origin, were we to insist on a sandstone structure for the original one, how many "periods" should we have? An early Hindû period; a later Hindû period; a Muhammadan period; and a British period! So, until this age of discovery shall provide some tangible theory to the contrary, I will be content to regard this sandstone basis as coëval with the superstructure, and merely a favourable departure in the mode of constructing these old walls.

With the exception of those already mentioned, the architectural objects which still exist on Târagarh are few.

The Moslem and minor *durgahs* of *Baharam Shahid* and others are characteristic examples of Mughal architecture and that of earlier Moslem epochs. The gateway of the former is even an imposing structure, and near to this building, which the natives in a strange confusion of tongues persistently call *Pir-pâdri-ka-durgâ*, is a cemetery containing three hundred graves, in which the unsuccessful Muhammadan invaders of Târagarh are interred in regular lines. There are also a few fragments of sculpture in and near to the hamlet on this fortress.

The city of Ajmêr is in latitude 26° 26′ 30″, and longitude 74° 39′ 31″. It is 677 miles from Bombay and 232 by railway from Agra.

In the fortified buildings now called the Magazine I have already mentioned that we have an early Hindû building. It is at present heavily laden with lime, the result of countless coatings of whitewash, which have been almost successful in disguising its antiquity in the matter of filling up and completely hiding any carvings it may bear. The work of the subordinate magistracy or *tahsîl* is now carried on here, and this fine old building, which has been so ill-treated by the whitewashers, and labelled "The Tahsil," will, it is to be hoped, do good public service for many years to come. The gate of this "Magazine," which looks citywards, has been identified with that mentioned by Roe, and up to the window of which that gentleman was obliged to climb on scaffolding, in order to interview the Emperor Jahângir. If we except its enhanced extent, Ajmêr is much as Roe left it. The dam, or band, "whose head is made of stone, in show exceeding strong,"[1] near which he was encamped, and the bursting of which occasioned so much well-described danger, can still be traced. Indeed, nearly the whole range of buildings along the *Ana Sagar* existed in those days, and several existed long before. The *Daulat-Bâgh* and *Nurcheshmah* still flourish, though in less degree than in the days of the "Conqueror of the Universe."[2] I made it a point to examine these most interesting scenes, and feel confident that no traveller's time will be wasted in doing likewise; on the contrary, it is most refreshing to visit these objects, long since described by a man like Sir Thomas Roe, in whose Journal the state of India in the seventeenth century is so vividly presented.

In addition to the remains already enumerated, I found an exquisitely-sculptured tomb of white marble; the perforated

[1] Journal of Sir T. Roe (see extract further on).
[2] *Lit.* Jahângir.

screens surrounding the sarcophagus of this tomb are equal in workmanship to anything I have seen, and the marble is of the finest quality. In plan this mausoleum is a quadrangle of 15′ 1″ sides, or 60′ 4″ in circuit. It is 9′ 5″ high above its marble platform, or basement (which is itself 4′ 6½″ high and 128′ in circuit), thus making up a total height of 13′ 11½″. There are two minârs in a more or less broken condition in front of the tomb. A curious feature of this sepulchre is that the steps leading from the ground to the floor of the marble platform are not in front of the main entrance, but on one side; no reason for this is obvious.

There is another tomb in the same enclosure (the *Ajmêr Sarâi*), which I afterwards heard was that of a Nawâb, Abdulla Khân, originally of Banda, in the North-Western Provinces, whose wife is entombed in the sepulchre of white marble above described.

Sir Thomas Roe, ambassador of James I., arrived at Ajmêr on 23rd December 1615, and on the 10th January 1616 presented himself at Jahângir's court and delivered his credentials. The following passages are extracted from Sir Thomas Roe's Journal, and as they possess a local interest I have inserted them here.

Jahângir, at the time, lived in the fort now called the "Magazine," and the attendants on his court seemed to have lived in extemporised houses outside the city wall, in the space between the Daulat Bâgh and the Madar hill. When Jahângir left Ajmêr for Mandar, he gave orders to set firê to all the *Lashkar* or camp at Ajmêr, to compel the people to follow, and the order was duly executed.

"The King comes every morning to a window, looking into a plain before his gate, and shows himself to the common people. One day I went to attend him; I found him at the window, and went up on the scaffold under him. On two tressels stood two eunuchs, with long poles, headed with feathers, fanning him. He gave many favors and received many presents; what he bestowed was let down by a silk, rolled on a turning instrument; what was given him, a venerable, fat, deformed old matron, hung with gymbals, like an image, plucked up at a hole. With such another clue at one side in a window were his two principal wives, whose curiosity made them break little holes in a grate of reed that hung before it to gaze on me. On Tuesdays at this window the King sits in judgment, never refusing the poorest man's complaint; he hears with patience both parties, and sometimes sees with too much delight in blood the execution done by his elephants. *Illi meruere, sed quid tu ut adesses.*"

This gate is probably the principal entrance to the Magazine on the city side, where there is a window on each side, such as Sir Thomas Roe describes.

The next description is of a place, generally called the Nur chashma, at the back of the Târagarh hill. The fountains and tanks are in a ruinous state, and the place can only be reached with difficulty, as of yore.

"The 1st of March I rode to see a house of pleasure of the King's given him by Asaf Khan, 2 miles from Ajmere, but between two mighty rocks, so defended from the sun that it scarce any way sees it, the foundation cut out of them and some rooms, the rest of free-stone, a handsome little garden, with five fountains, two great tanks, one thirty steps above the other. The way to it is inaccessible, but for one or two in front, and that very steep and stony, a place of much melancholy delight and security, only being accompanied with wild peacocks, turtles, fowl, and monkeys, that inhabit the rocks hanging every way over it."

Sir Thomas Roe also visited the Daulat Bâgh, whither he had been invited to supper by Jamal-ud-din Hassen, a man whom he describes as possessed of more courtesy and understanding than all his countrymen.

14.—NÂGAPÛRÊ, NÂGOR, OR NÂGA DÛRGA.

From Ajmêr I struck across 85 miles of the Mârwâr country in the direction of Bîkanîr, *i.e.*, north by west, in order to visit Nâgor, or, as it is generally spelt, *Nâgaur*, an old Mârwârî city, hitherto absolutely unexplored, as regards its archæological aspect, on account of its isolated position and the distressingly sandy roads by which it is approached. Nâgaur has not, that I know of, been visited by Europeans; certainly no one has described it, and indeed Europeans have little occasion to go near the place unless they are very desirous of raversing the Indian oasis, or of visiting Bîkanîr; the former is certainly not a popular undertaking, and the little Hindû State of Bîkanîr possesses still fewer attractions for Europeans.

The local authorities at Nâgaur, however, informed me that within their recollections some European merchants had passed through Nâgaur, carrying with them sundries for Bîkanîr, and from the names of this *farang* party, which they preserved, I conclude that they must have been Germans. But they wrote nothing of Nâgaur, and if they did, it has not been published. It may, therefore, be said that my visit to Nâgaur broke new ground.

Between Ajmêr and Nâgaur the country offered nothing of sufficient interest to induce me to make any halt, and with the exception of Pashkar, where there are a couple of fair stone temples, may be described as destitute of architectural features, whether antique or otherwise, albeit *sâtî*[1] tablets and pillars abound; but these are so common in Râjpûtanâ that one ceases to notice them after being a short time in the country, and I contented myself with impressions of the inscriptions on a few of the oldest examples.

At Kûchêra, about two marches from Nâgaur, I observed some stone circles, which measured from 12 to 15 feet in diameter, but the peasants informed me that their occurrence was due to a favourite recreation of the Râjpût youth called *tâhar* or *ewâro*. This game—the mention of which quickly divested these circles of a mystical, or indeed any other significance, and which may perhaps account for the origin of such circles in other parts of India—is played in the following manner: A sufficient number of large stone boulders (some of which would take a strong man to lift) are first arranged in a circle, and this circus is called *dhânnî*, "a small village;"

[1] Literally "faith." Destruction of human life by means of fire, whether the victim be a deluded Hindû widow or a nonconformist to Christianity, seems to have been regarded as "an act of faith" in several parts of the world,—to wit the *auto-da-fé* happily long since abolished. We had thought that sâtî, also, had been abolished, but I read in a Panjâb print some weeks ago that this dreadful ceremony has been performed by a *thâkûr's* representatives in Uniâra, a dependency of the Jaipûr State. The offence, for as such is this "act of faith" now regarded by our legislature, was promptly reported to the Governor General by His Excellency's Agent for Râjpûtâna, and the culprits have been duly punished.

the young shepherds then heave smaller stones into this mock village, and he whose stone falls nearest the centre of the circle, where, it is said, the fattest cattle of the village are kept, gains a certain advantage over his fellows. I understand that the game is of very early origin, and it is locally said to be one of the *líla*, or field sports, of the pastoral incarnation Krishna.

The foundation of the city of Nâgaur is popularly assigned to Rai Bisal, who was sent for that purpose by Râja Prithvî Singh of Delhi, the last Chohân emperor, and the following is the local tradition concerning its founding. I translate from a manuscript prepared for me by the Pîrzâda, or chief Mûllah, of Nâgaur :—

"The spot on which Nâgaur city is built, was originally wild forest and waste lands. There was a tank named *Bal Sumad*, or 'the Solar Ocean,' on the height near the *Ackhas* gate. There was a great jungle here, and *Pírthví* Râja of Delhi, when he heard about this jungle, sent those of his horses which were lean and sick to this spot in order that they should graze and become strong; the grass of these pastures being famed for its beneficial effects on the condition of horses. The shepherds of a city named Karm Nâgaur, situated 3 *kos* from Nâgaur (*sic.*—that is the present Nâgaur), used to send their animals here for grazing purposes, and it happened that, out of these, one ewe was separated from its fellows and gave birth to a lamb under a tree. A wolf came to eat the lamb, but the ewe fought with the wolf like a lion, and the latter running away, the lamb was saved and the shepherd took back the ewe to his flock. This singular occurrence was reported to Râja *Pírthví*, who thereupon sent Sardâr Rai Bisal, of the Pandrali estate, with orders to build the city of Nâgaur and drive a peg into the ground with a view to secure a firm and safe spot, as His Majesty considered the augury of the conquest of the ewe over the wolf as most propitious. In obedience to his sovereign's commands Rai Bisal went there and commenced erecting a fort and a city, and named the latter Nawa Shahar, or Nâgor, and both these names are still used. The date of the foundation of the city is 808[1] Saka Samvat, and Rai Bisal lived 60 years here in the

[1] According to local tradition, Rai Bisal was 19 years of age when charged by the last Chohân emperor to found Nâgaur, and, as Rai Bisal is said to have lived in, and governed, Nâgaur for 60 years, he must have retained his trust under the Ghaznî kings of Dehli long after the empire had passed from the hands of his former sovereign Prithvî Râja, who only reigned 22½ years altogether. This change of masters accounts for Rai Bisal's change of religion from Hindûism to Islâm.

time of Huzrut Hamid-ûd-dîn Rihâni, who came from Rihân and whose shrine is on a tank. Huzrut Hamid-ûd-dîn Nâgauri had come in the lifetime of Hamid-ûd-dîn Rehâni, while there was no Muhammadan there, and hence these two men were the first Musalmâns who visited Nâgaur.[1] He (Hamid-ûd-dîn Rehâni) it was who first inculcated there the doctrine of Islâm, and converted, amongst others, Rai Bisal to the Muhammadan faith. Rai Bisal was thence called Sultân Zirak and his agent was named Rai Lâl. He also erected a mosque.[2] During this time Huzrut Khwâja Mohizz-ûd-dîn [*sic.*] went to Ajmêr and Shahâb-ûd-dîn Ghorî to Delhi. Huzrut Chishti, whose shrine is at Nâgaur, was descended from Huzrut Umar, and was the successor of Huzrut Khwâja Mohizz-ûd-dîn[3] of Ajmêr. He came to Nâgaur in Samvat 1232, about 607 years ago, and died on 29th of Rabiul-Akbar 663 (A.H.). The door and the compound of the shrine were rebuilt by Muhammad Akl, son of Tughlak Shâh, in 630 A.H. Shams-ûd-dîn Ghorî[4]—was king at the time when Huzrut[5] Chishti lived. The great mosque of Shams Khân was built by that Khân, who was governor of Nâgaur, during his incumbency in the reign of Shâms-ûd-dîn of Delhi."

The above account is interesting in spite of the juggling phenomena which seem to be inseparable from the founding of Eastern cities. But, before dismissing this tradition, let us avail ourselves of all the information it contains, for the skeletons of these stories are often genuine before they are embellished with miraculous attributes by countless generations of Brâhmans and Bhâts.[6]

[1] The first two Musulmâns at Nâgaur were both called Hamid-ûd-dîn, one being surnamed *Rihâni*, with the title of *Qadi*, and the other simply *Nâgauri*. They are said to have been missionaries from Arabia and to have propagated the faith of Islâm here a few years after the foundation of Nâgaur by Prithvî Râjâ's agent, Rai Bisal.

[2] After the conversion of Rai Bisal to Muhammadanism, he built a mosque. That near the Kotwâl is pointed out as the veritable mosque of Bisal; but, I suspect, the present *masjîd* has been so much restored that it may fairly be called a renewal.

[3] Who was thus contemporary with Sultân Shahâb-ûd-dîn Ghorî.

[4] =*Iltitmish.*

[5] This prefix of *Huzrut* does not signify "royalty" when applied to religious celebrities. To Khwâja Husên Chishti, the descendant of Atarkin, tradition assigns the beautifully-sculptured gateway which leads to the tomb of Atarkin, a popular Muhammadan saint. On the summit of this gateway I found a Persian inscription of the Tuglak emperor Muhammad, son of Tuglak Shâh, dated in A.H. 630.

[6] Bhât, in Râjpûtâna, means a high-caste bard; elsewhere the term is a reproachful one, and generally signifies "an avaricious beggar" or "pander of low caste."

First, then, it would appear that certain persons in the Chohân court were desirous, either from party or personal motives, that a city should be founded on this particular site: hence the invention of the auspicious omen which was sure to meet with their sovereign's attention; for, in those dark ages, when the emperor's progenitor was devoutly believed to have had four arms and a fire origin, superstitious credulity would naturally preponderate over common sense.

Secondly, the tradition furnishes us with the *exact date* of the foundation of Nâgaur, which date is again checked by the lapse of time between Rai Bisal's imperial charge and his death.

Thirdly, that, with the exception of a single tank, nothing existed here prior to the year 808 S., as the tradition distinctly states that the place was a mere pasture.

Fourthly, that the name has nothing in common with the *Nâgarvansee* ("Ophidian race") or serpent worship; but that it is derived from a superstitious national custom then much affected by all sects on founding new cities, *viz.*, *Khīl gâdne*, which may be translated in the infinitive "to insert" (as in the earth) or "hammer down a rod."[1] Different versions of the same ceremony are related with regard to the second foundation of Delhi.

The original *bhâsha* name of this city, I am informed by certain Brâhmans, was Nâga *Gad*,[2] and, on the recollection of the above tradition growing fainter among the people in process of time, this name gave place to the simpler one of *Nâgor* (or *Nâgaur*), from *nâga* "snake" and और *aur*, which signifies "locality" or "region." The name, then, as it now stands, may be rendered "The ophite region."[3]

[1] In order to pierce *Shesh Nâga*, "hundred-headed serpent," which is supposed to support the world.

[2] Or *Nâga-garh*, which would be the same as *Nâga-durga*, *i.e.*, "Nâga fort."

[3] So far I have endeavoured to show how the people of Nâgaur account for the present name of their city, but these remarks can, of course, only refer to the spoken (*bhaka*) Hindî of comparatively modern times. The original Sanskrit form, as shown in the inscription which I discovered, was Nâgapûri.

Since the above was written, I have conversed with General Cunningham upon the subject, and he is of opinion that the initial *p* of *pûri* is commonly omitted in the modern rendering of such names. In that case we should have, admitting this elision (if I may be allowed to call the absence of a consonant an elision) *Nâgaure*, which again would easily become *Nâgaur*.

Serpent worship is *not*, nor perhaps has it ever been, performed here—except indeed to the ordinary extent practised throughout India on the festival of *Nâga pânchmî*. On these occasions five charcoal, or red-paint, strokes, representative of the five nâgas, are drawn outside the people's dwellings, and laved and anointed with offerings of milk, curds, and clarified butter.

The busy city of Nâgaur, with its battlemented walls, massive bastions, ornamental and lofty gates, and handsome buildings, both *intra*- and *extra*-mural, is eminently picturesque from all aspects; but more especially so from a couple of miles to the south-east, for here the ground is considerably higher than that on which Nâgaur is built, and the city is, by force of perspective, spread out, as it were, at the spectator's feet. From the gilded spires of the temple of *Mûralidhar* and the lofty towers of Akbar's mosque, to the humblest dwellings which, confusedly crowded together, always seem toppling over, yet never fall, all is exposed to view,—a grand view truly, and one which bears a strong contrast to the inhospitable, sandy wastes of Mârwâr, which stretch on every side as far as the eye can discern, and are wholly unrelieved, save by occasional outcrops of rocks and boulders, or weird, parched, and thorny-looking trees of khêr (*Acacia catechu*), khejra or karila (*Prosopis spirifera*), and bhabul (*Acacia arabica*), all of which are dwarfed in their growth, and afford no shade for the weary traveller in this desert.

The total circuit of the city walls I found, on measurement, to be 22,899 feet. The longest wall of this circumvallation is to the south, and runs from east by south to west by north; this single wall is 9,906 feet long. The next longest wall is that on the north side of the city, and running in a similar direction to the above; this wall is 9,296 feet long. Next in order comes the wall to the east, which runs from north by west to south by east; this wall measures 3,172 feet in length. The shortest wall is to the west, runs in a similar direction to the last-named one, and is 1,525 feet long.

Measured at the *kangras*, or battlements, the city wall

is 2 feet 6 inches in thickness, but at base it is 5 feet thick. It varies considerably in height, being generally highest towards the south; but 17 feet is the mean of several measurements which I made, and the general height of the gateways is from 25 feet to 30 feet. There is a curious projection towards the west of this walling, where it quits its direct course and forms a peak or promontory; the occurrence of the Nâkhas *tâl*, a large tank, within the city just here obviously accounts for this irregularity.

There are, altogether, thirty very massive bastions around Nâgaur, besides the abutments on either side of each gateway.

There are six city gates, three of which are in the southern wall, one in the western wall, one to the north, and one to the east. That in the centre of the southern wall is called the Jodhpûr gate, to the right and left of which (as one enters) are the Ajmêr and Nakhâs gates respectively. Near the centre of the northern side is situated the *Mâya* (or *Mauj*) gate. In the north of the western wall is the *Nâya* gate and a little to the south of the eastern wall is the Delhi gate.

The principal building here, in point of size, is the fort. This edifice measures exteriorly 1,600 feet along its southern battlements, and here there are nine bastions. Along its eastern battlements the fort measures 1,200 feet and has five bastions; north 1,150 feet, seven bastions; west 1,101 feet, also seven bastions. The walls are very massive and are built of two thicknesses, one rising above the other. The outer wall stands 25 feet above the ground, and the inner one 25 feet above the summit of the outer, or 50 feet above the ground. As each wall is 12 feet 4 inches thick, the total width of these ramparts, where they join together, is 24 feet 8 inches. This thickness, however, terminates above an elevation of 25 feet, though I reckon the scarped bevel, or slope, of the outer wall, as it graduates downwards, must add at least 6 feet to the entire thickness of wall; so that its width at base would be quite 30 feet 8 inches. The inner wall is built perfectly vertical, and, having no slope, does not diminish in thickness, and is, therefore, full 12 feet 4 inches across at top. All the bastions rise just 10 feet above the ramparts, and are thus 60 feet above the ground.

I will endeavour here to enumerate the principal objects in the Nâgaur fort, commencing from its furthest limit inside, and that most distant from the entrance gateway. Here is the handsome fountain which I found from its inscription to belong to Akbar's reign. It has seventeen jets, and is surrounded by a *chaupar*, or courtyard. To the north of the fountain is a room in which those in charge of this part of the fortress sleep, and further north there is a *tîrdawâlî*, or "hall of three walls," in a fine little garden, which is commonly used as a lounge. North-east of this fountain is a *bâradari*,[1] a handsome, painted hall, with numerous glazed and decorated panels; the walls of this building are beautifully *chunâm*-plastered.[2] Hence to the north of west is a *kachêri*, or "law court," now disused, and in front of which is a *baitka*, "lounge;" and to the north stands the *Ranvâs*, or "queen's abode," which is closed in all round and now also in disuse. To the north of the *kachêri* is another *bâradari*, on the façade of which are, tolerably well modelled in plaster, several images of elephants, horses, and other animals. These buildings are divided by a large *chogan*, or "parade ground," which is situate between the *kachêri* and the last-named *bâradari*.

Near the *Sûraj pol*, or "gate of the sun," is an old temple; passing through a *khîrkî*, or "postern," we come to another disused *kachêri;* further south is a mosque, which the attendant Mûllah states to have been built by Akbar, but which I found, by an inscription discovered inside, to have been erected by his grandson Shâh Jahân.

As is the case with the city, there are six portals to the fort of *Nâgaur;* indeed, they (the fort and city) resemble each other in more respects than one, for the masonry (*i.e.*, a base, about 4 feet high, of carefully-dressed sandstone blocks, with little

[1] Literally a "hall with twelve doors." But the term is applied to any building with four walls, and it is immaterial what number of entrances it may contain.

[2] Chunâm plaster is much used all over Râjpûtâna, but the industry properly belongs to Jaipûr, where it often resembled marble so closely that one is deceived. It is executed at the rate of 5 rupees per 100 superficial feet, *i.e.*, an area of 10 feet square.

or no mortar, supporting a superstructure of conglomerate boulders, filled up with thin slabs and a small proportion of mortar) in both cases is the same.

The road of this fort passes through it in the following way: Entering at the principal gateway, which is on the east, and proceeding to the westward, the visitor, after a time, turns alternately to the south-west and north-west, and hence to the south of west; after which, proceeding ten paces to the south, he turns abruptly to the west and reaches the last gateway; as it must be understood that there are gates at each of the angles above described. Having described the windings of this ramp and the bearings of its gates, I will proceed to name the gates in the same order: 1st, *Sari pol;* 2nd, *Bichl* (or *Dhûsa*) *pol;* 3rd, *Kachêri pol;* 4th, *Sûraj pol;* 5th, *Dhûpi pol;* and 6th, *Râj pol.* There are two *khîrkîs*, or posterns, the position of one of which I have given, and the second is near the *Râj pol.*

After having examined this city carefully, I have no hesitation in saying that quite half the area enclosed by the city walls is unoccupied, and that considerably over a third of the buildings here are in absolute ruin.

There are only two really noteworthy temples at Nâgaur, though one of these is virtually a double temple, *i.e.*, two separate shrines and buildings within the same enclosure; moreover, not only are the shrines separate, they belong to two sects of Hindûism, differing so widely from each other as the Saivites and Vaishnavites. Unusual as this may seem, the lingam of *Mahâdêva* and the statue of Krishna as *Mûralidhar* or *bansi-dhar*, "the flute-holder," are side by side: encompassed by the same enclosure, spanned by the same pillars, and entered from the road by the same gateway.

Another feature of this temple (or rather these temples) is, that Sivâ's symbol is in a pit or well, sunk 25 feet below the floor-level and approached by twenty-five steps.

I made a careful plan[1] of this fine temple, which is approached from the north by a very good arrangement of three large

[1] For plan see Plate XI.

halls, or courtyards, leading into each other by three moderate flights of steps, and divided by three long, covered-in galleries, which can be used as dwellings for the priests or monks[1].

The other temple is called *Barmâyanjî-ke-mandar.* On the occasion of my visit to Barmâyan, situated to the north of the Ganges, some time ago, I was much puzzled to account for the name of that village, nor could any one there tell me anything about it. But I was more fortunate at Nâgaur, and learned that *Barmâyan* is the name of an obscure goddess, one of the *Yogini*, among the *dei penates* of the Hindûs.

The courtyard of this temple is full of sculptured pillars, and is presided over by a Brâhman woman, who is considered by the *bhagats* ("votaries") of the shrine, a representative of the goddess Barmâyan. In this temple I found three inscriptions, one of which is, however, completely destroyed, having been intentionally gouged with some sharp instrument along the lines of writing. The other two are in better preservation, though hardly sufficiently perfect to afford connected readings.

The following is all that I have been able to make of these inscriptions :—

No. I.

[2]*Samvat 1618 brikhî Jêth-badi 13 Sanauare Koṭ nâgaire* (or *Nâgaure*) *Samas Khân.*

And, at end, what I make out to be some gifts to the temple by mahâjans of six mishals of something worth 16 rupees a mishal, and again 8 tolas of *thunari* (?). But they are both in some ungrammatical *bhakha.*

No. II.

[3] *Samvat 1659 brikhî Chetramâs Sukalpakh tithi tredara.*

I can also read *Sagatji*, probably a proper name, and again "one pair" or *Jodi ;* again, *Mâtâji ;* and I thought I could read in 11th line *Sri Santri.*

The above are merely tentative readings of these inscriptions, which are too much broken to deserve reproduction in

[1] This temple possesses a long Sanskrit inscription of 39 *slokas*, in which the place name is twice given as *Nâgapúri.*

[2] 13th day of dark fortnight in May 1618 S.

[3] 3rd day of March 1659 S.

facsimile. The temple of Barmâyan is said to be much older than these inscriptions, which only bear dates and commemorate certain donations to the temple.[1]

As Plates XI and XII will give detailed plans of both these temples, it will only be necessary to supplement them by the following measurements of the heights of the various objects, architectural and other :—

Double temple of Mûralidhar.

Height of *sikri* of Mûrali-dhar shrine . .	50′
,, ,, cupola, Mahâdêva shrine . .	35′
,, ,, inner enclosure of both shrines .	15′
,, ,, outer ,, ,, courtyard . .	10′
,, ,, inner partition guarding each sanctum	3′
,, ,, 1st gallery from temples . .	25′
,, ,, 2nd ,, ,, ,, . .	...′
,, ,, north wall at entrance gate . .	15′
,, ,, *chhatrîs*, or gilded minarets, at ends of northern gallery . . .	45′ each.
,, ,, staircases leading to above (2nd courtyard)	10′

Pillared temple of Barmâyan.

Height of flat-roofed temple	40′
,, ,, each carved pillar	9′
,, ,, basement of sacred *tûlsî* tree . .	4′ 2″

The famous cave at Nâgaur is claimed by the Hindûs as a place where the most rigorous austerities (*tapasya*) of their religion were formerly performed, and by the Muhammadans as that which afforded a subterraneous passage from Rihân for the Arabian missionary Hamid-ûd-dîn.

Whatever its origin may be, I found two inscriptions in this cave, one in Hindî and the other in Arabic. The first is dated in *S. 1603 bri-she-posa badi 5*,[2] and is, apparently, a pilgrim's record. The second, though in beautifully formed and cut Arabic characters, is dated with Hindî numerals in a most unusual fashion.

The cave leads out of a hall 53 feet long from north to

[1] For plan of Barmâyan temple see Plate XII.
[2] 5th day of dark fortnight of December 1603 S.

south and 27 feet wide east and west, the walls throughout being 2 feet thick and built of stone in the ordinary way. This hall contains twenty pillars, each 3 feet 4 inches in girth, fourteen of which support a walled-in gallery, which runs along the south-west and half of the northern sides of the hall, and sixteen of which are disposed in two rows from east to west at the southern end of the hall, and hold up a covered portico, immediately under which, and let into the southern wall, are the two inscriptions. This piazza is 14 feet wide, as each of the inter-columniations is equal to the width of the gallery, *i.e.*, 7 feet, = 14 feet.

The height of this building externally is 13 feet 6 inches and internally (from floor to ceiling) 9 feet 9 inches; the difference between these two dimensions allow for a roof 1 foot 6 inches thick, and a screen-wall around the terrace, 2 feet 3 inches high. The hall is entered by an ordinary wooden door, 5 feet high and 3 feet 4 inches wide, which is at the northern end of the eastern wall, which encompasses the whole.

Passing through the hall transversely to its opposite (south-west) corner, we approach the cave, and, lifting a large stone slab, with which the orifice is kept covered, enter (or rather descend into it, for the first portion of the cave is a square well 1 foot 9 inches across and 6 feet 5 inches deep) an underground chamber, 5 feet 3 inches long by 4 feet 6 inches broad, to the north of which another *khirkî*, or small standing door of stone, 1 foot 6 inches square, leads into another chamber, 5 feet 10 inches high, 5 feet 3½ inches long, and 4 feet 6 inches wide; this again communicates with another compartment, which is unfortunately closed fast, and the religious prejudices of the natives totally preclude an entrance being effected. However, by remaining a considerable time, until the eyes became accustomed to the prevailing gloom, I discovered a third door which measured 2 feet 1 inch square.

The Hindûs say there are, in all, seven such chambers. I have already given the Muhammadan version of the cave's extent.

The Hindû religious establishments of minor importance are very numerous within and without the city of Nâgaur, and I have the best authority for stating that the church lands or grants of free sites (*maafi*) for the construction and maintenance of temples, or the residence of Brâhmans, are more extensive in this than in most other provinces of the State of Mârwâr.

Wander about in the neighbourhood of Nâgaur in almost any direction, and you will pass countless cosy dwellings (*Sûkh dhâm*) held in perpetuity by *Bâbâji* the Brâhman; fertile fields of which he eats the fruits, or the *Mindar* at which he rings bells and anoints with red-lead alike idols and idolators, to his heart's content.

Those who know that Nâgaur, with a total population of about 6,000 souls, supports 131 temples, will follow me when I call it very religious—nay, tolerably priest-ridden. I caused lists to be made of the temples at Nâgaur, which, shortly after my arrival there, struck me as being very numerous, by my own servants, who visited them along with some local assistance I was able to procure; but the following table only includes the most noteworthy of those temples, the others being mere names, and many are even nameless:—

Name of Temple or Builder.	Dimensions.			Situation.
	Ht.	Lth.	Bth.	
1. Built by Khîchar Thâkûr .	20′	76′	50′	East of Nyadarwâza.
2. „ Sâdhû community .	50′	20′	25′	Ditto ditto.
3. Vishnû Pâda Mandar . .	20′	100′	25′	South ditto.
4. Built by Brâhmans . .	30′	40′	15′	Ditto ditto.
5. Ditto do. . .	25′	30′	18′	In Mahala ditto.
6. Built by Piti mahâjan .	25′	44′	12′	Ditto of Brâhmans.
7. Dharm sála . . .	20′	25′	15′	Ditto ditto.
8. Thâkûrjî ka Mandar . .	25′	75′	20′	Ditto ditto.
9. Dharm sâla . . .	15′	30′	15′	Ditto ditto.
10. Mahâdêva temple . .	13′	25′	25′	In Mahala of Brâhmans.
11. Nameless (roofless) . .	12′	100′	30′	Ditto ditto.
12. Built by banyas . . .	20′	30′	15′	Ditto ditto.
13. Thâkûrji ka Mandar . .	30′	40′	40′	Ditto of potters and lac bracelet-makers.
14. Sadhû's rest-house . .	20′	30′	30′	
15. Ditto do. . .	20′	0	25′	Ditto ditto.
16. Ruined and disused temple .	20′	28′	0	Ditto ditto.
17. Thâkûrjî ka Mandar (Vaishnav)	35′	50′	20′	Ditto ditto.
18. Built by mahâjans . .	25′	30′	15′	Ditto ditto.
19. Temple of Sanicharjî . .	15′	0	0	Ditto ditto.

Name of Temple or Builder.	Dimensions.			Situation.
	Ht.	Lth.	Bth.	
20. Temple without name or idol	30′	50′	50′	In Mahala of potters and lac bracelet-makers.
21. „ of Thâkûrjî . .	20′	60′	41′	Ditto ditto.
22. Râm Deola . . .	15′	30′	20′	Ditto ditto.
23. Nameless, with four-armed figures	31′	50′	50′	Ditto of talc-workers.
24. Ditto do., lingam .	25′	60′	45′	Ditto ditto.
25. Built by banyas (very old) .	20′	35′	100′	Ditto ditto.
26. Nameless, without idol .	10′	20′	18′	Ditto ditto.
27. Ditto do. . .	30′	0	20′	Ditto ditto.
28. Built by Kûmhar (potter) .	30′	35′	25′	Ditto ditto.
29. Temple of Raghûnâth .	25′	50′	15′	Ditto ditto.
30. „ ruined and nameless .	20′	0	30′	Ditto ditto.
31. „ of Mahâdêva . .	25′	60′	35′	Ditto ditto.
32. „ Thâkûrjî, built by a Khâti (carpenter) .	25′	30′	20′	Ditto ditto.
33. „ Kûmhâr community .	25′	50′	40′	Ditto of Kumhars.
34. „ Râja Bakht Singh .	36′	0	43′	Between Jodhpûr and Nakhas gates.
35. „ Bhenrojî .	15′	14′	13′	Ditto ditto.
36. „ Parasnâth (Jain) .	25′	100′	60′	East of Bakht Singh's temple.
37. „ Thâkûrjî . .	30′	80′	40′	North-east, Jain temple.

The principal mosques at Nâgaur (not counting such prayer enclosures, with a mere screen-wall to the west, *ķiblah*, as are found in large numbers) are as follows :—

Name of Mosque or Builder.	Dimensions.			Situation.
	Ht.	Lth.	Wth.	
Juma Masjid	15′	40′	15′	In front of Nakhas gate.
Pathânî	15′	25′	26′	In Mahala of Brâhmans.
Nameless (large dome) . .	40′	31′	22′	Ditto Charans.
Built by Kasais (butchers) .	20′	30′	18′	At Nakhas gate.
Disused and ruined . . .	15′	26′	13′	In Mahala Nakhas.
Ditto do.	20′	13′	14′	Ditto ditto.
Built and used by hawkers .	15′	30′	30′	Hawkers' quarter.
Sipais' mosque	13′	18′	15′	In Mahala of Kaseras.
Mosque of Doldha of Bâf community (weavers) . . .	15′	12′	12′	Ditto ditto.

Name of Mosque or Builder.	Dimensions.			Situation.
	Ht.	Lth.	Wth.	
Mosque of Shêkhs . . .	15′	0	0′	In Mahala of Kaseras.
Ditto Pathâns . . .	15′	25′	20′	Ditto ditto.
Ditto Armourers . .	11′	30′	21′	South of Nakhas gate.
Ditto do. . .	20′	25′	25′	Ditto ditto.
Ditto Sakheras . .	20′	26′	0′	Ditto ditto.
Ditto dealers in lac . .	35′	0	17′	Ditto ditto.
Ditto Mughals . .	30′	42′	20′	Near Shams Masjid.
Ditto Shams Khân . .	See detailed account of this five-domed mosque further on.			Shams tâl.

The private dwellings at Nâgaur are also worthy of a passing note, as they belong to the middle period of the Mughal Empire, and possess three long inscriptions. The largest building is called Thâkûrjî-ka-makân, and measures 38 feet from north, to south, 65 feet from east to west, and 28 feet high. Its walls are 2′ 6″ thick, and it contains five compartments or rooms. Above its entrance gateway (which is 8′ 6″ high by 6′ 10″ wide), and about 10′ above the street, are two long inscriptions, carved in raised Persian letters, which are very well formed.

The second building is called *Raijî Lori-ka-makân* in the spoken *bhâkha* of the place. It is 22 feet wide from north to south, 70 feet long, east and west, and 25 feet high. The walls here are also 2′ 6″ thick, and the rooms six in number. The inscribed gateway is smaller than that of the above building, as it measures only 6′ 10″ high and 3′ 7″ wide. The inscriptions which I found here are let into the wall immediately above the door, and are somewhat inferior to the last named as regards workmanship.

There are altogether seven tanks at Nâgaur: 1st, *Partâp Sâgar*, near the *Nya darwâzah*, to the west of city; 2nd, *Lâl Sâgar*; 3rd, *Bakht Sâgar*,[1] hewn out of solid rock, by Mahâ-râja Bakht Singh, who spent the greater part of his life at

[1] Near the *Bakht Sâgar* is the tomb of Hamid-ud-dîn Rihâni, whose subterraneous passage from Rihân to Nâgaur is traditionally held to account for the Nâgaur cave by the Muhammadans.

Nâgaur. This tank is on the north side of the city, and approached by three gateways leading from the city gardens through the outer circumvallation, whence steps lead down to the tank. These openings (or gateways) have been closed up of late years by the authorities, and therefore the tank is only accessible from without; 4th, *Ginanî tâl*, near which is a small inscribed arch; 5th, *Shams tâl* (vulgarly called Sambas tâl by Hindûs) situated to east, and immediately in front of the Shams Masjîd there is a beautiful sheet of water, in the centre of which, and resting on a small island, is the tomb of Shams Khân, the builder of this fine old mosque; 6th, *Jharâna Rânî ke sâgar*; and 7th, *Nakhâs tâl.* Of these tanks, the 1st and 3rd are extramural; the 2nd, 4th, 5th, 6th, and 7th being inside the city wall.

To the east of the city are some scattered and straggling remains, which consist principally of tombs and irregular mounds, covered with building materials. Conspicuous among these are the remains in an old mosque, or rather the two minarets of one, as, at present, but two tall minârs are extant. I was unable to find any walls to this mosque save a small disjointed piece to the east. But the ground here has risen considerably from various causes, and, no doubt, excavations would disclose walls of some sort, though they would necessarily be very low down. There is also a gigantic grave of a *naogaja pîr*, or saint, whose stature is said to have been 9 yards! These are, however, common in several parts of India.

Owing to the feuds and pitched battles constantly indulged in by the Mahârâja Bakht Singh (who, it should be remembered, lived the greater part of his life at Nâgaur), the city walls and battlements were often broken down, and these breaches were, I believe, repaired with materials obtained by the demolition of mosques. According to accounts rife at Nâgaur, Aurangzêb himself never destroyed more temples than did Bakht Singh mosques, and this may—indeed does—account for the numerous Arabic and Persian inscriptions which I found built topsy-turvy into the main circumvallation of the city,—some upside down, some diagonally, and others so that the lines of writing stand up vertically.

The following are the most important of these inscriptions :—

1. Gateway inscription:

"This Gateway was built (? or repaired) in the reign of Muhammad, son of Tughlak Shâh Sultân, in middle of month Shahbân A.H. 633."

2. Inscription of a mosque in fort:

"There is but one God, and Muhammad is the Prophet of God.

"This mosque was built in the time of Aba-ul-Zafar (? Muzafar) Muheed-ud-dîn Muhammad Aurangzêb, who is the son of great kings. May God ever preserve his kingdom and country! The mosque was erected by Chand, son of Hamid, resident of Nilgarh. Its date is 9th of Muharrim-ul-Haram, 1071 H."

3. Inscription over arch leading to Genani tâl:

"Built in 1011 by Râja Râm Singh, son of Râja Amar Singh, Rathaur, when Muhammad Alam Nasir-ud-dîn, son of Alamgir the great and good Musalmân king Aurangzêb reigned over the country."

4. Inscription on fountain in fort:

"The foundation of this fountain was laid in the reign of Jalâl-ud-dîn Muhammad Akbar (may God keep his country for ever!) by Hasam Quli Khân."

5. Inscription in Akbari Masjîd:

"In the time of Shâh Akbar this mosque was erected in 985 H."

6. Inscription on isolated building on fort:

"Inasmuch as this building was erected without a roof by Hazarat Sultan-ul-Arfin (*i.e.*, king of pious men) Qazi Hamid-ud-dîn, Nagoré, I, humblest of men, Muhammad Nasir, built the roof on the 2nd of Zilhij, 1047 H."

In the early part of this account I have mentioned the period, extending over 200 years, at which Nâgaur was governed by a Khânate, deputed by Shams-ud-dîn Iltitmish, and it only remains to describe the interesting old mosque here which was built by Shams Khân, the founder of this family of Khâns. I allude to the Shams Masjîd—the Shams tâl (vulgarly called Sambas tâl by Hindûs) immediately in front of the mosque is also due to Shams Khân. Of this curiously-constructed mosque, a plan to scale will be found in Plate XIII. I found twenty-three old Hindû mason's marks, two short inscriptions (or constructive memoranda), and a large Arabic inscription, in this building.

Like the great mosque at Ajmêr, the details of the Shams Masjîd are curiously Gothic in appearance,—for example the sanctum. For a drawing of the principal one see Plate XIII.

As will be seen from the elevation of the *Shams Masjîd*, it is a long building, in front of which is a spacious, walled-in courtyard which leads through a *ḥûjra*, or "pavilion," at its eastern end. To the *Shams tâl* there were formerly steps down to the water's edge, but these have long since fallen into the lake. The mosque has altogether five entrances, two of which are closed up. But the features of this mosque distinguishing it from most others that I have seen, are its five cupolas and triple floor. Mosques commonly have three domes to correspond with the three prayer niches or sanctums. The triple floor, or two additional false floors of this example, are almost unaccountable.[1] The only way in which I can account for the additional or false floors at the ends of this building is that they were designed to accommodate a larger congregation than was intended by the original architect. Against this solution it may, however, be urged that these two floors at the ends bear no appearance of being constructed subsequent to the original mosque in which they occur, as there is a radical difference in the ends of the buildings occupied by them, from the centre portions, *i.e.*, whereas in that portion connected by the three principal central cupolas the final ceiling is supported upon single pillars reaching from floor to ceiling, in those ends spanned by the end cupolas, and where the double false floors occur, a double series of columns has been found necessary—the 1st series, 7′ 11″ high, reaching to below, and supporting, the false floor; the 2nd series, 6′ 1″ high, resting upon the false floor and supporting the common roof. Now, it is at least highly improbable that the entire pillars, similar to those

[1] The only other instance which I have seen where false floors have been built, is the temple of Brindaban, and here the resemblance is only partial.

supporting the three central arches, could have been dismantled to allow of the construction of these intermediate floors as an after-thought, for in that case, unless the common ceiling was very dexterously upheld by temporary beams, a collapse of the ends of the building would have been imminent.

The centre arch, or principal sanctum, of this remarkable mosque is 9′ 7½″ high and 2′ 3″ deep. Resembling strongly a statue niche in a Gothic chapel, it is elaborately fluted by nine successive minor niches, which, together with the floral pointed termination at top, give it a highly ornamental appearance. The two minor niches are mere recesses, with sharp corners, 8′ high and 1′ 8½″ deep. To the right of the principal *meḥrâb* just mentioned, is a very well built, ornamental *mimbar*, or "pulpit," 6′ 10″ high, having a *zina*, or interior winding staircase, by which the eminence is gained. Inside this *mimbar* is a perfect little stone chamber, or *tâk*, 4′ 8″ long, 2′ 9″ broad, and 4′ high, in which to store the theological books, *e.g.*, Kurân. Immediately to the east of this pulpit, and in the gangway of the main entrance, is a grave-like mound 2′ 7″ high. I was for some time at a loss to account for this ill-placed cairn; but a close examination convinces me that it is sepulchral, and for its sole accommodation the *musallah*,[1] or "prayer floor," has been deliberately dug up.

In addition to the five entrances to the Shams Masjîd there are two more narrow passages at the ends, only[2] 2′ 1″ broad, which lead by two series of stone steps up to the highest *minârs* or *mazînas*. These staircases are not spiral or winding until the final roof of the building is gained, but consist of

[1] The *mussallah* is sometimes divided off into oblong spaces by alternate compartments of white and black marble slabs, each barely sufficient for one man to perform the genuflections necessary to Muhammadan prayer on. In such cases (*e.g.*, the great Jumma Masjîd of Delhi, built by Shâhjahân) the parti-coloured slabs serve to divide the congregation in much the same manner as do our pews. But in the Shams Masjîd no such provision has been made. A plain stone floor, however, extends outside for a width of 11′ 8″ along the frontage of the mosque.

[2] The irregularities in the constructive details of this mosque are well exemplified by the difference between this pair of *zînas*, or "stairs," that to the north end being 2′ 1″ wide, while that to the south is 2′ 4½″ in width.

two distinct flights each; the first reaching the false or intermediate floor, and the second leading on to the common roof, whence winding staircases leading to the *mazîna*, or crier's tower, can be entered.

The mosque is much ruined, the worst parts being to the south; and the centre or principal cupola is completely fallen in. As the plan[1] will give all the dimensions of this building, it will only be necessary for me to state here the elevation of the different parts.

The central main entrance is 32′ 10″ high, and the four doorways that flank it (two on either side) are 23′ 3″ in height each. There is an oblong projection behind the mosque screen in the neighbourhood of the principal sanctum, which was evidently constructed to allow for the recess of that *meḥrâb*; its height is 13′ 6″. The two towers (*mazînas*) at the ends of the edifice, from which the *muazzin*, or "preacher," called the congregation to prayers, are each 50′ in height. The ceiling of the mosque is 14′ 7″ in height; but, in addition to this, the roof is 2′ 4″ thick, so the complete height of the body of the mosque is 16′ 11″. The height, taken from outside from the ground to summit of the façade, is, however, 38′ 2″ at the centre, where an angular pediment rises above the battlements. On either side of the pediment, where the frontage is necessarily lower, it measures 29′ 6″ from the courtyard-level to its crown. The result of this vast difference between the total façade height and the interior ceiling dimensions, is the absolute concealment of all the domes of the mosque when viewed from the east. These battlements and this pediment are practically the first landing on the ascent to the *mazînas*, and are themselves attained by steps from the roof proper (composed of a very narrow strip around the domes).

The centre cupola is raised on eight minor columns, each 5′ 5″ high, and only divided from the eight lower main ones (14′ 7″ high) by an octagonal arrangement of architraves 10″ high. The octagonal portion of the cupola being now completed, the architect's next work was to reduce the whole

[1] See Plate XIII.

to a circle, and, finally, to a conical apex; this has been done by first reducing the octagonal ring above the second tier of pillars to one of 16 angles, and then to one of 32, whence it was easily further reduced to 64 sides, and so on to a true circle. Hence we have a height of 21′ 8″ from the floor of this mosque to the extremity of the base (or octagonal portion) of the centre cupola. Now, the cupola is unfortunately fallen in, and so I cannot give its precise *total* height; but, allowing the same height as its octagonal basis to the entire spherical dome (which must have been about the proportion, judging from the remains), the whole cupola must have been 14′ 4″ high: add 2′ 11″ for the thickness of the dome, and the result is 31′ 9″ for the height of the crown of the dome from the ground, or 6′ 5″ less than the angular pediment in the centre of the façade before mentioned. This being the proportion which the centre dome bears to the frontage, it is no wonder that the dome is effectually concealed from the east. The smaller domes bear the following proportions to the massive *kangra*, or battlements, by which they also are quite hidden from the eastern aspect of the building.

I have already stated that the ends of this building are supported by a double tier of pillars, with a false floor or partial, middle-storey-like platform between them; but there are no small pillars in the cupolas here, nor in those immediately flanking the central dome, which, alone of the five, is built with an octagonal base, supported by small additional pillars. The interior ceiling being 14′ 7″ high, the whole length of the building, and the total interior height of the four minor cupolas 24′ 11″ above the mosque floor, we have only to add the thickness of the domes, *i.e.*, 3′ (or 1″ *in excess* of the central dome), to ascertain the total height of this portion of the mosque, *viz.*, 27′ 11″; and, as the *kanguras*, or battlements, are 29′ 6″ above the courtyard[1] just here, the domes are less than the battlements by 1′ 7″. The diameter of the centre cupola internally is 19′ 8″, and that of the other four 17′ 6″.

[1] The courtyard is on an exact level with the mosque *musallah*, or "prayer floor," which indeed exceeds the front of the building and stretches for 11′ 8″ into the courtyard.

The square pillars throughout the building are 1′ 2¼″ thick.

Outside the *Mâya* gateway is a large enclosure containing several tombs of Muhammadans of note, and in the midst of this *ḥazîra* stands a superbly-carved gateway of stone, popularly called *Atarkin ke darwâzah.*[1] But, though tradition assigns its construction to this Muhammadan saint, of whose antecedents I have endeavoured to give an epitome in the early part of this account, I found on the summit of this gateway and right behind the uppermost member of the building, where it was quite hidden from view, a Persian inscription of the Emperor Muhammad, son of Tughlak Shâh, which is dated in 630 A.H. But the gateway was only *repaired* by that prince.

This remarkable structure measures 41′ 10″ high to the top of its white marble battlements; but its two minarets are 11′ 6″ above the battlements, and, therefore, 53′ 4″ from the ground. Entering the building from the south, one can pass right through to a garden behind or to the north; but if an ascent to the top of the gateway is desired, either of two narrow staircases, 2′ 1″ wide by 5′ 3″ high at entrance, leading into the east and west bastions, must be selected. The main opening which leads into the garden, where also there is a mosque, is only 7′ 3″ high and 3′ 7″ wide, as is the case with so many Muhammadan buildings which have disproportionately small entrances. There are two gateways in this portion of the building, to the north and south ends of a passage leading through it. The walls here are very massive, being 4′ 9″ thick, measured at the principal entrance, and at the postern 3′. There are three flights of steps, with three landings, ere the summit of the main building is gained; one of these flights is placed outside the building for want of room inside (see Plate XIV). A fourth flight conducts one up to the *chhatris*, or pinnacles, which are at the corners of the large projections, or angular bastion-piers, of this gateway. There are four

[1] This Atarkin is a very popular saint and venerated by Hindûs and Musalmâns alike: the former are often seen in great excitement near the tomb of Atarkin which is guarded by this grand gateway.

storeys to each pinnacle tower, supported on four pillars each; so that the towers contain sixteen pillars, each pillar in the first or lowermost storey is 6′ 9″ high and 3′ 8″ in girth, those of the second storey 5′ 10″ high and 3′ 3″ in girth the third 5′ and 2′ 6″ respectively, and the fourth 5′ and 2′ 6″ respectively.

Behind the façade, and resting on the lower part of the gallery, are three domes. This part of the building the main roof on which the dome rests, is only 33′ in height, the centre dome is 12′ and the end ones each 6′ high; so that, measuring from the ground to summit of the centre dome, the total height is 45′, or 3′ 2″ in excess of the moulded façade, notwithstanding which the dome is invisible from the front, or south, of the gateway, owing to the circumscribed space in the courtyard and the exigencies of perspective.

In the body of the building there are two chambers for sentries or pilgrims, 7′ 5″ long, 7′ 3″ wide, and 5′ 3″ high. Excepting a beautiful promenade behind the battlements, seats in the pinnacles, and the two chambers above described, there is no accommodation in the gateway building.

The walls, or piers, of this building are very massive indeed, and those in the centre are cleverly arranged in four blocks of solid masonry, in order to afford a good strong stay for the main building.

The gateway of Atarkin is magnificently sculptured in every part, and the geometrical patterns and other objects moulded thereon are of every imaginable form. The elevation in Plate XIV will present this graceful façade more readily than any description; I would only call attention to the centrifugal arrangement of the carvings over the main arch, as differing from the straight parallelism of other examples.[1] All is in the same light-yellow limestone of which the seven arches of the Ajmêr mosque are built, save the battlements at summit, which are of white marble. A large ostrich's or bustard's egg hangs suspended by a chain from the apex of the arch, and is accounted one of the sacred objects of the place.

[1] This arch is noteworthy as one of the first constructed in India. Its faults are obviously the result of inexperience.

A tradition exists that the building was commenced by Atarkin himself, but finished by his heir, Khwâja Hûsên Cheshti, who carried the architect, Shêkh Abdûl (mentioned in the end of the Tughlak inscription which I discovered here), on his back to Medina seven times in order to take the plan of a similar edifice there; the architect having forgotten the dimensions six times on his return to Nâgaur.

Regarding the people at, and within a radius of 100 miles of, Nâgaur, I observed their habits with great interest, but fear they have little to recommend them; indeed Mêrwârîs and Mârwârîs (I have as yet only observed the northern portion of the last-named race) are alike characterised by few admirable qualities.

Everything that is bad in the Râjpût has been attributed by observant authorities to their habitual and inordinate use of opium; but there are certain unhappy propensities in the northern Mârwârî's nature with which opium has nothing to do, *e.g*, ostentation, indolence, and coarseness of sentiment. His bravery (or, I should say, that of his forefathers, for I am writing of the men in whose company I am at present) has been proved beyond doubt by history; but his treachery has also been proved by the same agency. The very settlement of the Kanauj Rathors in Mârwâr was effected by base ingratitude and murderous treason on their part.[1] From a small party of fugitives from Kanauj in A.D. 1212, "the Rathors, the issue of Seoji, spread over a surface of four degrees of longitude and the same extent of latitude, or nearly 80,000 square miles, in less than three centuries after their migration from Kanauj, and they amount at this day," (about 1820 A.D.) "in spite of the havoc occasioned by perpetual wars and famine, to 500,000 souls."[2] They, or rather the mixed population in Mârwâr, have managed to

[1] The story of the murder of the Pâliwal Brâhmans of Pâli by Sêvaji (the progenitor of the Rathors of Mârwâr) is well known to the people. The Brâhmans entertained him hospitably and gave him lands, as a return for which Sêvaji took advantage of the *Holi* festival to assassinate his benefactors and appropriate their country. The story will also be found in Tod's Râjasthân, Volume II, page 12, of the reprint.

[2] Tod's Râjasthân, Volume II, page 19, of the reprint.

bring under cultivation considerable tracts of poor and sandy soil; two capitals, *i.e.*, Mandor and Jodhpur,[1] besides other cities, towns, and villages, have been formed. But we now have all, I think, that can be said for our Mârwâris.

15.—GÂVAN.

Gâvan, or *Gowan*, as it is also pronounced, lies midway between Nâgaur and Ûstrân, and is a village with an agricultural and nomadic population of about 300 souls.

On the western bank of a large tank, called Ellûra Tâl, to the east of the village, I discovered a tower of stone, 25′ high, the exact purpose of which I could not find out. I think it is not a Râjpût *sâti* cairn, for these seldom attain a height of 25′, and I have never seen them even half so high.[2] On the other hand, it would be difficult to say what *else* it is, unless it be a stone stûpa, and, therefore, I dug into it diagonally, but without any result; but I suspect my excavations were made too low down in the monument, and perhaps, also, not sufficiently deep; but it was laborious work removing the huge stones, and, as my halt at Gâvan was only of two days' duration, I stopped operations after arriving at the base from a little below the centre.[3]

The middle portion of the tower slopes inwards, and the general outline gives a tolerably perfect concavo-concave figure; this is, no doubt, due to the stones having dropped from the centre, and spread out the conformation of the base; those employed towards the acme are larger and even, partially dressed stones, and have consequently adhered to the building with greater tenacity.

The base of the tower is built of large undressed stone

[1] Nâgaur itself was at one period of its history the capital of Mârwâr, or "the region of Death," as Tod calls it. He is, however, wrong; for *Mâr* is no substantive, but simply the root, or imperative mood, of the verb "to strike."

[2] The tallest *sâti* tower that I have seen (excluding *chhatris* and *deolis*, is 12′ high, and stands near the village of Ren or Ran; besides, all such towers have steps by which the top of the cenotaph is gained. The tower of Gâvan has no trace of such steps.

[3] As promised to the headmen of the villagers, I carefully replaced the stones which I had removed from this ruined tower.

boulders and blocks of roughly-squared red sandstone intermixed; the middle portion contains inferior material (hence its decay), which again improves towards the crown of the building.

16.—MANDOR

Is situated one march to the north of Jodhpur.

The population of Mandor is composed almost entirely of *mâlîs*, or gardeners; but while the proper occupation of a *mâlî* is naturally horticulture, numbers of men of the *mâlî* caste find employment in the Mandor quarries as stone-cutters, or *sangtârâsh*. But those who cling to their own profession are by no means idle, for Mandor, and indeed Jodhpur itself, is very numerously studded with gardens; I know of no other place where, within the same area, so much attention is paid to gardening operations. Numerically speaking, the gardens of Mandor and its neighbourhood (including Jodhpur) are surely unequalled elsewhere; for, besides others, we have *Lâl Sâgar bâgh* and *Wazir Bahsh bâgh*, a pair of fine walled-in gardens, the first deriving its name from that of a lake within it, and the second from that of a Muhammadan who formerly held office in the Jodhpur State; these gardens are about 1½ miles to the north-east of Mandor.

The third garden is nearer at hand, and is named *Râmjî bâgh;* the fourth is called *Dewân bâgh;* the fifth, *Phûl bâgh;* the sixth, *Partâp Singhjî Khokrî;* the seventh, *Moti Singh bâgh*, containing a palatial building whose roof has fallen in; the eighth, *Bal samand;* the ninth, *Chhal bâgh;* the tenth, *Sûr Sâgar bâgh*, near the Residency; the eleventh, *Jahavira bâgh;* the twelfth, *Kailâna bâgh;* the thirteenth, *Byalai bâgh;* the fourteenth, *Machhia bâgh;* the fifteenth, *Nandla bâgh;* the sixteenth, *Sarak bâgh;* the seventeenth, *Rânî-dân bâgh;* the eighteenth, *Baria bâgh;* the nineteenth, *Metha-nadi bâgh;* the twentieth, *Jarachi-jî bâgh;* the twenty-first, *Kagga bâgh* (and the cenotaphs of the inferior queens of Jodhpur are here); the twenty-second, *Rai bâgh;* the twenty-third, *Bhiya bâgh;* the twenty-fourth, *Nijar bâgh;*

the twenty-fifth, *Wazîr Ali bâgh;* the twenty-sixth, *Chand-sûkh Kûa* (so called from a well inside); the twenty-seventh, *Chanka bâgh;* the twenty-eighth, *Tagas-Sâgar bâgh;* the twenty-ninth, *Chûna-baria bâgh;* and another nameless garden in which I saw a plentiful crop of poppies, on the banks of the *Nigadrî nadî*, now quite dry,—making thirty large gardens, besides others of smaller dimensions which I was unable to see, within an area of a few miles, those few miles being in one of the least fertile and most drought-stricken localities in India. An infinity of labour is required to irrigate and tend these gardens, and hence the large number of *mâlîs* in this part of Mârwâr; several villages are entirely populated by them, *e.g.*, that near the pair of gardens first mentioned, where there are about 350 gardeners' dwellings; near *Sûr Sâgar*, where there must be 400 houses of *mâlîs;* and Jodhpur itself contains nearly 1,000 houses of this caste.

Besides Junagarh, or the ancient fort of Mandor, the archæological remains here consist of a number of richly-sculptured stone cenotaphs. Of these monuments, seven really fine examples exist in the neighbourbood of Mandor: six in contiguity with the garden called *Moti Singh bâgh*, and one on an elevated plateau beyond Junagarh; and less than a mile from Mandor, called *Panch Kûnda*, or *Pash Kûnda*, on account of a supply of sacred water (contained in five tanks) which rises just here to a phenomenal elevation, being but a few cubits below the surface of the plateau, which is several score of feet above that of the surrounding country. This place is one of general pilgrimage for Hindûs, but no fair is fixed, and bathing in the waters, which are somewhat tepid, and most probably supplied by some mineral spring, is deemed almost as praiseworthy as bathing in the Ganges itself. This natural plateau is composed of rock, and is almost as level as though it were a stone floor, prepared artificially. I have before stated that there is one noteworthy cenotaph, on *Pash Kûnda;* but there are several others of more modern date and modest execution, and here, as well as with those below lying to the north-west of Moti

Singh's garden, the most insignificant *thâras*[1] were designed to perpetuate the most famous names, and thus a low mound of *débris* and mixed stones, of all shapes and sizes, contains the memorial buildings of the *Rio Râja's Chondo*, *Rae Mal* and *Jodha*, the founder of Jodhpur. Originally these *thâras* were mere shed-like buildings, uninscribed and unembellished in any way; but even these have been suffered to tumble together in a shapeless mass! A little further south stands the richly-sculptured monument of *Rio Ganga*, and this is the oldest cenotaph that has retained its four walls *in situ*. I say four walls advisedly, for the roof, or spire, has long since disappeared. The stone-carving on this building is of the most elaborate kind, as an cxamplc of which may be mentioned the rich *bas-relief* running round it and representing elephants, horses, &c., drawing war-chariots, which is truly fine;[2] the manner in which the floor offered by the stone plateau for a foundation has been *packed up* with stones so as to form a level surface to build upon, is also very characteristic of the shifts that have to be resorted to in a stony country.[3]

Quite close to *Rio Ganga's* cenotaph has been erected, a few generations back, a small temple, enclosed by walls, and on examining this temple, which is built almost entirely of the ruins scattered about in all directions, I discovered two inscriptions, of nine and seven lines respectively: the former was let into the floor, along with several other flat stone flags, to form a foot-path into the temple; and the latter, into the lower part of the right wall as one enters, half underground, and, if I remember rightly, upside down. I also found another

[1] *Thâra* is the name given to the humblest description of cenotaph, and it is built of simple boulders, or partially-dressed stones, and much resembles, both as to size and shape, a small peasant's hut. These *thâras* are, however, roofless. The *chhattri* is a trifle more costly, being, as its name imports, a "canopy" resting on pillars and generally raised from the ground on a platform; it is approached by steps. The *déoli* is the grandest description of memorial building, often three storeys high, with several chambers, staircases, and terraces; each very richly carved. These *déolis* have steeples, and are erected on the same lines as a *mandir*, or idol temple, only that such temples are dedicated to divinities, and the *déoli* to the mortal whose memory it preserves.

[2] See Plate XV.

[3] For front and side views of *Rio Ganga's déoli*, see Plates XV and XVI.

short inscription built into the hall *behind* this temple, which records the Samvat date 1266 (A.D. 1210).

I caught sight of a couple of letters of the first-named inscription which fortunately appeared above the sand and rubbish covering this foot-path or causeway, and on its being cleaned, I had impressions taken of those parts that were uninjured.

The second inscription had to be dug out of the earth, which, on account of its low position on the wall, nearly covered it. It is much defaced.

The third inscription is broken off and lost after the first two lines, which merely record a date very imperfectly.

Further still to the south of what may be called *Panch Kûnda* plateau, are a large number of monuments of the *chhatri*, or canopy, type. These are all erected in memory of the true queens[1] of Mârwâr, those of the females of an inferior class belonging to this Court being at Kagga near Jodhpur. The largest of the queens' cenotaphs on Panch Kûnda is that of the consort of the Mahârâjâ Mân Singh; this *chhatri* contains thirty-two pillars, is handsomely carved, and, in a kind of votive chapel in the centre, bears an inscription which sets forth his queen's name as the *Kachh Wâha Jî*,[2] and the date of her demise in V.S. 1882 (A.D. 1826). I found no inscriptions on the other *chhatris*, save one or two very modern ones.[3]

As I have before stated, the plateau in which these monuments are built is of bare stone, so that no foundations have in any instance been excavated, and the architect has been obliged to level his foundation by packing up the hollows with stone on which the base of each building rests on its own weight, apparently without any collateral support. All these *chhatris* are built of highly-wrought stone, which unfortunately is plastered over, and whitewashed plaster and whitewash are the banes of a large portion of the architecture in this part of India; much good carving is completely marred by

[1] Pat-rani.

[2] This is merely the tribal name, but the only one by which this queen, who came from Jaipûr, was known.

[3] For this group of cenotaphs see Plate XVII.

attempts at coating it over with a glazed, stucco-like preparation that is so successfully employed in parts of Jaipûr, and in those chambers of Government House, Calcutta, called the "Marble Hall;" but this latter work was done by men brought from Madras, and as the walls and pillars there are quite plain, the white glaze appears to great advantage. But in several buildings in Mârwâr, and elsewhere, rich ornamental carving, and also figure sculptures, are covered over with the preparation and immediately rendered paltry-looking. I have often been at a loss to define between stucco ornamentation and stone-carving, or *bonâ fide* sculpture. A single neglected *chhetri*, of red sandstone, retains its stone-sculptures clear and uncovered with stucco, and it is by far the most pleasing example in consequence. Collectively, these buildings on the Pash Kûnda plateau look very well, and I photographed the group from the east, and that example, uncovered with stucco, is roofless and somewhat in the background of the group; it is also naturally of a darker stone, and can easily be distinguished in Plate XVII. The *chhatri* of Mân Singh's queen is the largest, and placed near the centre of the group.

There are only two small mosques at Mandor, and one of these (that in the town) is in ruin and disuse; so that there is only one at which prayers are said. This mosque, named *Masjîd Ghûlâmî Khân*, stands a little to the east of the Panch Kûnda remains above described, among a heterogeneous group of Muhammadan buildings, none of which are very old. The *dargâh* of *Tanna Pír* is conspicuous in this assembly, both on account of the high veneration in which the fane is held, and for some handsome sandalwood carvings with which it is decorated. It was erected during the reign in Mârwâr of the Mahârâjâ Mân Singh. The other large tombs here are those of a Pathân named Ghulâm Kalandar Khân (one of the oldest), and of Gamna Ghâzi. This tomb is entered through a fine stone Mughal gateway around which some religious Musalmâns live. Though there is but one mosque here, it amply suffices for the Musalmân community of Mandor, there being only five true believers out of a total mixed Hindû population (within the town) of 300. In the midst of these Muhammadan buildings I found a very old *satí* tablet dated in Samvat 1224, which, if the Vikrama Samvat be meant, is equal to 1168 A.D.

The principal cenotaphs, and indeed the most important objects at Mandor, are near the garden of Moti Singh, and stand on the same level as the town of Mandor. These buildings stand in an almost straight line, which runs from north to south, and to the west of the more modern cenotaphs which exhibit a marked retrocession in the builder's craft. Why is it that modern indigenous buildings in this country are inferior to the old ones? The same quarries that supplied material for the latter are close at hand, and certainly not exhausted, and the Mârwâr State is not, that I am aware of, less wealthy than of yore. Is it because the art of architecture is extinct? Perhaps this is not so much the cause of this deplorable inferiority, as the want of *appreciation*, in the natives of to-day, of really conscientious work. The modern building gaudily embellished with crude colors or covered with stucco the white reflection of which well-nigh blinds the spectator on a bright day, is far more esteemed by the present generation of natives than the magnificent buildings of solid sculptured stone reared by their forefathers. As an illustration of the above it is only needful to state that a building of the former description (the cenotaph of the late Mahârâjâ Mân Singh) is daily tended, cleaned, and ardently admired, whilst the six older and really handsome monuments first named are wholly neglected; indeed, they are offensive to the olfactory organs when their upper storeys are visited. As to the present state of native public opinion regarding them, this will be readily estimated when it is known that a colony of *dhobís*, or washermen, inhabit and store their soiled clothes within these splendid remains. The vaults are also occasionally used as store-rooms in which the ashes of modern cremations are locked up until it is found convenient to bind them in an urn-like vessel and immerse them in the River Ganges; and the ashes occasionally have to wait a considerable time before they are conveyed to their last watery resting-place. They do not lie in state, as we understand it, but in a corner of a dark dungeon, densely crowded by bats. During my stay in Mandor, one of these sanctuaries (that of Râjâ Gaj Singh) was so occupied.

From an examination of the environs of Mandor, I conclude that the royal cremations, in memory of which these cenotaphs are erected (much in the same manner as were the *stupas* of old), were originally conducted on the elevated plateau called Panch Kûnda, until the reign of Rio Maldeo Singh, when the ceremony began to be performed on the spot near the garden of Moti Singh, which is the cremation ground to the present day, as the cenotaph of Rio Maldeo Singh is the earliest here. But this observation only applies to the reigning princes and their near male relatives; the legitimate and illegitimate wives are cremated on Pash Kûnda and Kagga respectively.

The earliest cenotaph of the lower series stands to the extreme south of the line of six, and is that of the Rao Râjâ Maldeva Singh, who reigned over Mârwâr from 1532 to 1584 A.D. He was a contemporary of the Mughal emperor Hûmâyûn. Of Maldeva it is related that he was sufficiently mean to plan the capture of Hûmâyûn, when that much-wronged monarch was flying from Sher Shâh, who had just seized his throne; the plan was happily unsuccessful, but nevertheless the base attempt would, doubtless, have lost Mârwâr to the successors of Maldeo, had it not been for the personal liking conceived by the Emperor Akbar for Rao Maldeo's son, Udê Singh, whom Akbar called the Mota Râja,[1] and of whom several local tales still exist at Mandor.

[1] It is quite possible that in translating *Mota Rájá* simply "the fat prince," Tod has lost a local idiom which puzzled me on first entering Mârwâr. *Mota Rájá* does certainly signify "fat prince," if translated literally, but *mota* in Mârwâr means "great," "good," "large," "extensive," "powerful," "potent," and such like adjectives. A Mârwârî will apply the qualifying word *mota* to a large city, a wealthy or powerful man, and even, as I have seen, to clear water; in fact, to him *mota* means simply anything that is excellent or praiseworthy. Besides, it is much more likely that the courteous Akbar would invent this title for Udê Singh, with whom he was pleased, in a respectful or polite sense, than as a reflection on his obesity. I therefore hold that *Mota Rájá* was meant by Akbar (who was not slow to acquaint himself with the national idioms of such distinguished courtiers as the desert king) as a regular title similar (and identical in significance) to that of *Mahárájá*, "great prince," and not "fat prince," which sounds much like ridicule, and even coming from the Emperor of India would be rude familiarity.

The *deoli* of the Rao Maldeva is inscribed over the door of the sanctum and also elsewhere about the interior. The records of later times are, however, unimportant; the inscriptions proper to the cenotaph are clear, and have been copied by means of impressions. But the chambers are dark, and so these could not be corrected or amended.

The second building, counting from the south, is the *deoli* of Râjâ Udê Singh,[1] the first prince of Mârwâr who bore the title of Râjâ, his predecessors having been called simply Râo. This cenotaph is also inscribed, and I have made out a portion of the inscription.

The third cenotaph, still following out the line northwards, is that of Râjâ Sûr Singh, who reigned over Mârwâr from[2] 1595 to 1620. It isinscribed.

The Râjâ Gaj Singh's *deoli* comes next (4th), and this is uninscribed, save in one place, up in the loft, where I found a proper name, which may, perhaps, be that of a pilgrim. But Gaj Singh was sufficiently well known without inscriptions, and so the builders of this fine *deoli* probably thought; but will his name and fame be equally independent of such records in the time that is to come? Of Gaj Singh we learn from Tod's Râjasthân that he reigned from A.D. 1620 to 1638.

The fine monument raised in memory of Râja Jeswant Singh, who reigned from 1638 to 1681, follows that of Gaj Singh, and is uninscribed.

The sixth cenotaph is that of Râjâ Ajît Singh, who reigned from' 1685 to 1725 A.D., and it forms the terminating link to this magnificent chain of buildings. It is profusely inscribed and marks the spot where sixty-four of his queens perished in the flames of Râjâ Ajît's funeral pyre. Ajît was the hero of the thirty years' war in Râjpûtâna, and finally died by the hand of his parricidal son.

If we are to judge from this cenotaph of Râjâ Ajît, there can be little doubt that architecture had reached a very high

[1] Udê Singh reigned over Mârwâr from 1584 to 1595 A.D.

[2] This interregnum was caused by the outbreak of the thirty years' war which ravaged Mârwâr from 1682 to 1712 A.D., and at the first few years of which Râjâ Ajît Singh was not permitted to reign.

point of excellence in Mârwâr 158 years ago, when it was erected. Though the carvings individually are no better than those on the old cenotaph of the Rao Ganga on Pash Kûnda, nor indeed than those on some others forming the line below, the design of Ajît's monument is larger and more grand than anything in the neighbourhood.

The deduction that I have been able to draw with regard to the general architectural characteristics of these commemorative buildings, is that the older spires are roundish on the outside in outline, that is, convex, and this convexity is generally more perceptible the older the example; a little later this spherical conformation disappears altogether and the sides are straight or obeliscal, and, later still, they tend inwards and become concavo-concave, and this hollowness increases the more modern the example. The *deoli* of Rao Maldeo Singh *versus* that of Râjâ Udê Singh (which stand side by side) will readily illustrate the above remark.

I went inside the tower of Râjâ Ajît's cenotaph, and observed three trellis-work props, formed of four wooden poles each, fixed into it at equal distances from base to summit. Should these be necessary as supports, I would strongly recommend the speedy employment of some more substantial and safe substitute.

To the east of this principal line of monuments are the more humble cenotaphs of the Râjâs Abhai Singh and Bakht Singh, and though the former was an energetic prince and able warrior, we can feel little regret that his name is only perpetuated by this little *thâra*; indeed, it would be well if his name could be wholly forgotten and expunged from the annals of Mârwâr, which record that Abhai Singh was a parricide. But, besides this prince, the memory of others is doomed to like neglect, *e.g.*, Bakht Singh, brother to the parricide, who also in his turn occupied the throne of Mârwâr, which he wrung from its rightful occupant, Râm Singh. This usurpation and the subsequent installation of Bejai Singh were the cause of prolonged civil war in Mârwâr just as that ill-fated State had emerged from the thirty years' struggle for independence with the empire.

The cenotaph of Bejai Singh is hard by, and is also a humble building, though considerably larger than the others in this line; it is closely surrounded by those of his sons and other relatives, *viz.*, Sûr Singh, Sher Singh, Savant Singh, and Pratâp Singh, none of whom ever reigned. Râjâ Bejai Singh's tomb is duly tended and watered; and prostrations are still made before a little wooden stool which serves to represent his throne, and which is carefully enshrined in the cenotaph.

Behind, or to the west of, the humble *thâra* of Bejai Singh is the *deoli* of the short-lived prince Chhatar Singh, the son of Râjâ Mân Singh, and it is a fairly representative specimen of modern buildings of the kind.

At the south-west corner of the *deoli* of Chhatar Singh I found a very interesting cairn, quite hidden from the common view by *jangal* and some meaningless old walls. This *chabûtra* is inscribed, and was built in memory of some affluent Thâkûr, who is styled in the inscription "Râjâ Bakhtâwar Singh, Kachh-waha of Jaipûr." The inscription is dated, and from the date I infer that this man must have been one of the Kachh-waha nobles who accompanied the founder of Jaipûr on his hostile mission against the Râjâ of Mârwâr, which proved so disastrous to him of Jaipûr. The *casus belli* in this case is said to have arisen out of some disputed rights of vassalage which the latter (Abhai Singh) claimed from Bikanêr, whose prince had succeeded in interesting Râjâ Jai Singh of Jaipûr in his favour. Many Kachh-wahas must have perished in that battle, which ended very unfavourably for Jaipûr. But a Kachh-waha monument within the enclosure, sacred to the *manes* of the Rathors, is certainly a curiosity. I had the *jangal*, &c., cleared away from this cairn.

There are here, besides the cenotaph of the prince Takht Singh, those of Bhumm Singh, Sirdâr Tai Singh, Fatteh Singh, and Bahâdûr Singh. These, however, are very modern.

What a change has Muhammadan influence wrought in India! Even into the proper names of her sons, words from the invader's language have crept. Such a name as Sher Singh is surely paradoxical, meaning, as it does, "Lion, Lion:" both words signify the same thing in different tongues. Again, BahÂdur, Takht, and Fatteh are clearly Persian for MahÂ, GÂdi, and Jai respectively.

Before constructing a cenotaph it is usual for the priests and others in charge of this cemetery (?) to enshrine the shoes or other relics of the deceased on a chair or stool in a temporary shed adjacent to the proposed site for the cenotaph, which should be erected exactly over the site of cremation.[1] The seat represents the presence of the departed, and is usually surrounded by the ordinary temple appurtenances, *e.g.*, *pûja*-bells, flowers, &c. When the cenotaph, or more permanent memorial, is ready, this temporary contrivance is removed. While at Mandor I witnessed this ceremony, as the foundation of a new cenotaph was barely laid, and I was then informed that it was a very ancient custom.

I have before stated that such names as Rao Chanda, Rao Raemal (or Rin Mal), Jodha, Abhai, &c., possess very humble *thâras*, but subsequent research has convinced me that these princes had not even these *thâras* erected with the object of preserving their memory, for those I have described as resembling small peasants' huts, are merely erected to facilitate cremation, and when it is intended to build a monument, these are demolished, and serve only to mark the position of the *sanctum* of such monument; thus, each of those great *deolis* must have been *thâras* at first.

I also examined the "old fort" *Jûnagarh* at Mandor, which Tod calls "Cyclopean." But all here appear to have suffered from the effects of an earthquake, and, with the exception of the very superior masonry exhibited in the walls that still remain above-ground, and a number of masons' marks, which I carefully collected and which may assist in determining its approximate age, these remains are not distinguished by any characteristics different from those of half a dozen old places in Northern India.

[1] This rule has, however, been slightly departed from in the case of Râjâ Jeswant Singh's monument, to the north-east corner of which, and detached from the building by a few feet, is the small enclosure in which the funeral pyre was lighted. But this is very unusual, and, owing to exigencies of space, for this Stupa is rather cumbersome.

I found a low pillared chamber on Jûnagarh, which is very dark inside and of solid construction; the sculptured figures it contained were not uncommon, nor indeed is any of the sculpture on this fort-mound. The stones of which the walls are composed are large blocks, very truly squared and raised above each other, perfectly dry, without cement of any kind. I also succeeded in finding one of the original gateways to the west, whose lintel is only 1′ above the *débris* level; the whole of the portal's framework below that being completely buried, and elsewhere the gateways are buried altogether. Locally the destruction of the fortress is attributed to the curse of a *Jogî*, or religious mendicant.

The characters which I found incised on various parts of the walls of Jûnagarh, but principally towards the western angle, are as follows :—

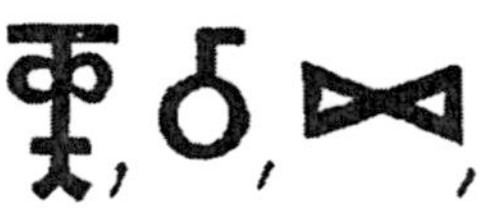 (two of this),  (two of this very large) 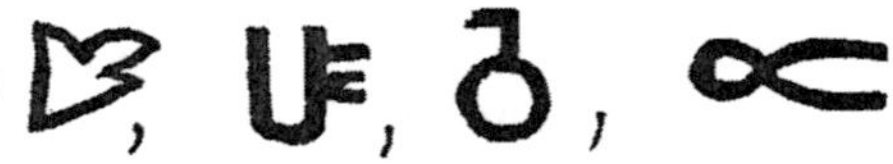 and  which last looks modern. These letters are generally very clearly and boldly incised, and are generally about $2\frac{1}{2}''$ high. The first may be a compound of *chh*, *k*, and *t;* the second looks like an Asoka *v* and *e;* the third is probably a mere symbol, or it may be a deformed *m* turned on its side; the fourth is not unlike an ancient *s*, with an additional flourish; the fifth a Gûpta *d;* the sixth is undoubtedly the numeral 90; the seventh appears to be meant for a leaf, and was probably cut by some idle mason who had nothing better to do; the eighth is probably a compound of *h* and some other letter;[1] the ninth an Asoka *v* and *a;* the tenth is the numeral 10, and the eleventh is nothing if not a modern Devanâgari *k*.

[1] This figure is incised on one of the stones forming the road which leads across the fort, and which was laid down quite lately as a relief work during the last famine. Here I found it, but its original position is not known.

At Mandor there are altogether seven temples at present in use (apparently quite modern), two or three of which are Jaina.

A gallery of colossi at Mandor contains sixteen figures, hewn out of a single natural rock, along the face of which a long shed, or gallery-like building, partially divided off into compartments, has been constructed as a shrine for them. Some of the figures are represented on horseback, and some are unmounted; all are colossal, and all are very poor examples of Hindû sculpture. They were executed during the reign of Râjâ Abhai Singh, in whose reign, also, the stone gateway in the town was erected. This pantheon, if we may call it so, is known to the natives as *Chhetis-karor-devaton-ka-sthân* (or *sal*); it is also called *Kâla-gora*. The former name is derived from the conventional number of idols that are supposed to have been hidden in this gallery and its adjacent temple by Abhai Singh during his Gûjrâtî campaigns. An excellent native drawing of the images is given in Tod's Râjasthân.

17.—JODHPUR.

With the unimportant exception of a few additional temples and residences—necessarily all modern—Jodhpur presents much the same appearance now as it did sixty years ago to Colonel Tod, whose ample description of the fortress, &c., may be seen in *Rajasthan*, Vol. I, Per. Nar., Chap. XXVII.

Few temples are to be found older than those built in the reign of Râjâ Mân Singh, and at the instance, we are informed by the author of Râjasthân, of Deo Nâth, the high priest of that prince. This Deo Nâth, it would appear, was instrumental in placing the Râjâ on the throne of Mârwâr, not without a suspicion of having assassinated his predecessor.

18.—PÂLÎ.

This busy little city is one of the few places in Râjpûtâna that are built in the open plain. Pâlî was originally surrounded by walls and battlements, of which traces were visible in the early part of the present century, and, as Tod[1] informs us, Pâlî,

"like everything else in these regions, bore the marks of rapine; and as in the civil wars of this State its possession was of great importance to either party, the fortifications were razed at the desire of the inhabitants, who did not admire the noise of war within their gates. From the same feeling, when it was proposed to gird the sister mart, Bhilwara, with walls, the opposition to it was universal. The remants of the walls lend it an air of desolation." [1]

But I did not observe any traces of these walls, and Pâlî has long been regarded as open and unwalled. There are now two distinct localities at Pâlî, one being called *Jûna Pâlî*, or "ancient Pâlî," and the other *Pît Pâlî*, which in the dialect of these regions is held to signify "higher" or "modern Pâlî." The modern Pâlî has, however, in process of time, advanced considerably upon the ancient Pâlî, and hence it is that several of the oldest buildings are to be found within the precincts of the former locality.

In Jûna Pâlî I found eleven noteworthy temples, the oldest of which is a very handsome building, dedicated to Sôm Nâth, or "the Lunar god," as personified by Seva, who is here represented by his symbol the lingam, and attended by two small sculptured stone images of Nanda, the sacred bull upon which he rode.

This temple stands in a courtyard 76′ 9″ by 44′ 6″ in area. The total length of the main temple is 54′ 8″, and its width 25′ 8″. The courtyard, which is surrounded by a battlemented wall, 10′ 2″ high and 3′ 6″ thick, contains the following minor temples: counting from the main entrance to the courtyard the first on our right hand is the shrine of Annapûrna, or the "bestower of (daily) bread;" this temple is 25′ high, and its entrance is only 3′ 9″ high. Second is a *chhatri*, or canopied building, 15′ high, with a lingam of *Eklinga*. Third is the shrine of Ganpatijî, 20′ high; fourth that of Abdîvi, 21′ high: this is an open-pillared building to the east, whose sanctum is in its south-west corner. The fifth is an object which makes this temple, in common with the Jaina temple

[1] Personal Narrative, Vol. I, Râjasthân.

of Naolakha at Pît Pâlî, very noteworthy,—*i.e.*, the existence within its enclosure of a Muhammadan mosque. This little altar projects in relief from the western wall, into which it is built, and its two minarets top that circumvallation by 3′, as they are 13′ 2″ high, though the meherâb, or niched sanctums, are only 2′ 3″ high and 3″ deep. Religious toleration, it must be acknowledged, could not well exceed the limits to which it is carried in Pâlî, for here, as well as in the other five Jain temples, we find mosques inside the courtyard. Sixth is a small shrine dedicated to Sûraj Narain, "the Solar god," in contradistinction to Sôm Nâth, "the Lunar god," whose temple stands in the centre of the enclosure and is accounted the oldest temple in Pâlî. The minor shrine of Sûrâj Narain is 25′ high, of *sikarband* or obeliscal shape, and is entered by a door, 4′ 4″ high. Seventh (to the south-west of the principal sanctum) is a cylindrical building, 3′ 3″ high and 4′ 6″ in diameter, in which stands a trunk of a tree covered with silver and gold leaf, and supposed to be symbolical of Sanichar devata, who, along with Sûkh devata, is believed to have been an impromptu creation of Mahâdêva on one of his many nuptial expeditions, when that deity was in urgent want of attendants or bridegrooms. The week days Saturday (*Sanichar*) and Friday (*Sûkrwar*) are called after these *dei penates;* and barren women circumambulate the tower as a panacea for their woes. Eighth is a *tûlsî chabûtra*, or platform, 6′ high, on which the sacred *tûlsî* tree grows; this, too, is an object of worship. Ninth is the temple of *Bârabhojî*, 25′ high, entrance 5′ 8″ high.

The temple of Sôm Nâth stands on three tiers of elaborately fretted plinths, the first or lowermost being 9½″ high, the second 4½″, and the third 2″. The first hall of the temple is supported on sixteen pillars, each 5′ 10″ high and two more, of the same size, support the portico at the head of the eastern (main) entrance staircase. These pillars stand on shelf-like slabs, 3′ 6″ wide, which run all round and form seats in this chamber, and themselves rest on partitions of stone 5′ thick and 2′ 9″ high. To this we must add 1′ to the thickness of the seats in order to arrive at the distance from the floor of this chamber to its beams,—that is 9′ 7.″ But the floor throughout this temple is on an elevation of 4′ 3″ from the courtyard, which is again 1′ 6½″ above the road-level, as two steps, 9″ and 9½″ respectively, have to be ascended, and a formidable gateway, 5′ 3″ high, entered, before the courtyard is gained. The doorway that communicates from this chamber to the sanctum of the Sôm Nâth temple is 6′ 1″ high above its threshold, which is 1′ 5″ high. There are three stone bulls (*Nandî*) *couchant* in the first hall, the largest of which is 2′ 6″ high, the second 1′ 9″, and the third 1′ 2″. The lingam which occupies the centre of the sanctum is 1′ high, and a *sinhâsan*, or stone platform, at the back of the sanctum chamber stands 2′ high.

The first (eastern) chamber of the temple is crowned with a dome, whose summit cannot be less than 28′ or 30′ high, and a fine truncated obelisk rises over the sanctum chamber quite 50′ or 55′. I regretted much my inability, owing to an accident to my chemicals, to take some photographs of this temple, remarkable on account of its exquisite mouldings.

The other temples in Jûna Pâlî are those near the Kairiya-darwâzah, of which that of Gaurijî, a Jaina temple built by a *banya*, is the best. It is 100′ in length, 40′ in width, and 45′ high, and its walls are 2′ 3″ thick. Second, that of Kaireswar Mahâdêva, 30′ long, 20′ wide, and 50′ high, walls 2′ 6″ thick. These temples are surrounded by twenty-five *sâtî chhatrîs*, or canopied cenotaphs.

At the "Jodhpur gate" is a Sivite temple surrounded by ten others, amongst which is a Jaina shrine, 34′ in length, 14′ in width, and 20′ in height, walls 2′ thick. Also the temple of Raghû Nâth is here, which measures 100′ long, 80′ wide, and 40′ high, walls 2′ 6″; also the temple of Kâm Mâtâ, 70′ long, 40′ wide, and 30′ high, walls 2′ 1″ thick.

At the "Jhalawâr gate" is a picturesque Jaina temple, 101′ long, 20′ broad, and 33′ high, walls 2 1″ thick. To the west of this Jaina temple is a lake, 1 mile long, called Naojan, and having ghâts for bathers built. To the east of this fine sheet of water is another tank, on the banks of which is a temple called Dada-ka Mandir, and ten unimportant *chhêtrîs*. North of the latter tank is a Jaina temple, dedicated to Santi Nâth, 100′ long, 40′ wide, and 70′ high, walls 2′ 6″ thick.

At the *Sûraj pol* is another large temple of Gaurijî, who appears to be a very favourite deity at Pâlî. It is 120′ long, 30′ broad, and 50′ high, walls 2′ 9″ in thickness; and one of Thâkurjî (Vaishnava), 75′ long, 35′ wide, and 40′ high, walls 2′ 6″ thick. Also a temple of Sôm Nâth (Sivite), 80′ long, 30′ wide, and 45′ high, walls 2′ 4″ thick. Inside this temple are five small native temples, and near a *chhatrî* by this temple is a medium-sized tank, called Lauriya tâl.

In Pît Pâli, as I have before observed, notwithstanding its designation there are some fine old buildings. Foremost among these is the vast Jaina temple of Naulakha, for a plan of which see Plate XVIII.

All the Jaina temples which I have come across in Râjpûtâna have small entrances—disproportionately small for the buildings to which they belong; and this rule is strictly observed in this remarkable Jaina temple of Naulakha, which I will here endeavour to describe. Regarding the derivation of the name there are two distinct versions. According to one the temple cost nine *lakhs* of rupees, and hence its name; the second tale relates that it was built by a *mahâjan*, or merchant, named *Naval*, + *ka*, the genitive particle = *Navalka*, or *Naulakha*.

The temple, with its cloisters, stands in an enclosure, 250′ long from north to south, 140′ broad from east to west, and 12′ 6″ high. But, as this enclosure is surrounded by irregular and often temporary buildings and sheds, I have left it out of my plan, which commences with the cloisters proper, and thus shows the details of the temple on a much larger scale than it would be possible to do were the irregular outer enclosure included.

The main temple of Naulakha is formed of two distinct and almost equal parts, that to the north (front) being an open hall of forty-six pillars, each 11′ high, without walls, but with roof, 51′ long by 31′ broad; and the back portion to the north is a regular chamber, 40′ long by 31′ broad, with walls 2′ 6″ thick. The comparative thickness of these walls is owing to the *sikri*, or obeliscal spire, being mainly supported upon eight pillars, each 11′ high, which are arranged in a circular fashion inside the sanctum. There are four more pillars to the extreme north of the inner courtyard, and these with their roof form a canopy, which leads into the building next to that containing the well.

The sanctum of the temple has two more entrances to the east and west, which are likewise sheltered by canopies and supported on ornamented columns. The cloisters which surround three sides of the courtyard are also supported on pillars along their inner edge, the small pillars supporting the thirty-eight minor cloister-temples are each 7′ 6″ high, and those of the three larger cloister-temples are each 9′ high. The construction of these extensive cloisters will be clearly seen in Plate XVIII, and it is only necessary to say that the minor compartments are entered by doors 4′ high in the thirty-eight small cloister shrines and 5′ 9″ in the large ones, that they are crowned by *sikris* 30′ and 45′ high respectively, and that these steeples are double-steeples,—that is, small steeples run round the inner edge (facing the principal temple), and large ones round the outer edge of the courtyard, both being, of course, supported upon their respective cloisters; so that there are eighty-four steeples on the cloisters alone, and as the vanes of these are plated with gold at top, the appearance is somewhat dazzling.

All these cloisters contain small Jaina figures of the *Tirthankaras*, and all three entrances to the principal temple are 6′ in height; but as the ornamental threshold at foot of the sanctum entrance is 1′ 7″ high itself (the semi-circular projection being 3″ and the threshold proper 1′ 4″), the height of this entrance from the floor is 7′ 7″. Besides its gorgeous appearance, this temple is noteworthy for two very unusual features, the first of which it enjoys in common with the temple of Sôm Nâth here,—*viz.*, a mosque, which in this case is 20′ high, within the precincts of its courtyard; and the second is its strength or capacity as a defensive fort. The latter struck me forcibly on first entering the building, and a glance at the plan will, I think, confirm my impression. One must, however, bear in mind that the whole is again surrounded by another set of outworks; that all these out-houses and cloister shrines (which could easily be converted into barracks)—in fact every building—is only accessible *from within*; and that the solitary entrance from without is but 2′ 10″ wide and raised 2′ 2″ from the road-level by three steps and a wide threshold. Such an entrance would not require many men for its effectual defence.

Granting that small entrances are common to Jaina temples, it is seldom that one finds such very obvious traces of fortification (even to a strongly-guarded well) in the religious edifices of India.

The outer cloisters running round three sides of the court-yard are approached by three steps, which are in front of each shrine and betwixt buttresses, each 2′ 6″ high, and on which rest two pillars which support the common roof.

Like the temple of Sôm Nâth,[1] the Naulakha temple rests on fretted plinths and is elaborately carved in parts.

The mosaics in the front hall, or *ardha mandapa*, are interesting, both on account of their being undoubtedly indigenous, and of their excellence. The colours are yellow, black, and white, in well-arranged proportions, and the designs represent a variety of mystic crosses, or *swastika*.

19.—NADOLA.

(An old site in the Aravali Range, midway between Pâli and Raipúr.)

In the local traditions regarding the early history of this town, the following legend is preserved.

Originally Nadola was in the possession of a community of Brâhmans, and when Rao Lakhan the Chohân[2] arrived

[1] In the front chamber of this temple I discovered a Sanskrit inscription of 21 lines, of which, however, 17 are completely defaced, leaving only 4. But these contain the *Samvat* date 1200, and as the advent of the Rahtors in Pâlî is placed in *Samvat* 1212, the inscription, and likewise, of course, the temple of Sôm Nâth, must belong to pre-Rahtor times. All, save a letter in the corner of this inscription, was quite invisible, being completely covered over with innumerable coats of whitewash and stucco. But I had it cleaned, and regret much that it is in such poor condition.

[2] In the Râjpûtâna Gazetteer, Vol. II, p. 41, I find mention of a "Jodh Lakhan," who is called "the son of Prithvi Râj."

upon the scene, these Brâhmans employed him as *rekwâla*, or "watchman," of Nadola. A short time after his incumbency a certain cowherd reported to Rao Lakhan that a strange cow was wont to mingle with the cows which he (the cowherd) daily tended, and that after grazing on his pastures, she disappeared. In accordance with the Chohân's advice, the cowherd determined to pursue the unknown cow, and the next day, when she was on the point of running off as usual, he seized her tail and followed.

The cow led him into a mountain cave called Mangâra-ka-Jhânkar,[1] where he saw, seated over a fire, a little old woman who asked him whence he came and what he would have.

When the cowherd complained that he had not received any remuneration for the pasturage of her cow, she gave him a handful of golden wheat, which in his ignorance he straightway bartered for tobacco.[2] The merchant who became possessed of this wheat, happened to show it to Rao Lakhan, who, being versed in such phenomena, exerted himself to discover the source of the wonderful grain, and told the cowherd that when the mysterious cow was again homeward bound, he would accompany her to her lithic retreat. On the morrow, when the cow had finished grazing and was again ready to decamp, the cowherd, as before, seized her tail, and was in turn grasped round the waist by Rao Lakhan, and the three hastened away to the rocky cave, on arriving where, the same old woman whom the cowherd had seen on his first visit asked the Chohân if he had brought with him any offering for her shrine. "Yes," said Rao Lakhan, "I have brought the head of a dissatisfied man," and thereupon struck off the cowherd's head with his sabre and presented it to the crone, in whom he recognised the goddess "Fortune."[3] Fortune was gratified on receiving the cowherd's head, and bestowed Nadola and the outlying districts of God-

[1] Still pointed out 2 miles from Nadola.

[2] This is as the popular legend has it. But, as the tale refers to an early period, it is probable that tobacco, which was unknown in India before Mughal times, has been substituted for *opium*, which is said to have been introduced into India by Râjâ Qran.

[3] Lakshmî.

wâr upon Rao Lakhan, telling him that a *tanda*, or "caravan," of horse-merchants would shortly arrive with their wares, and that he was to sprinkle an infusion of sandalwood on the steeds, which would immediately change their colour, so that their owners would fail to recognise them.[1] With these horses the Rao conquered the Brâhmans of Nadola, his old employers, and ruled over Nadola and its dependencies (for Nadola was the capital of Godwâr), until an unlucky day dawned for him, when one of his servants of the *Nai* caste informed him that a woman of rare beauty daily visited the city. Rao Lakhan stationed himself in his *bara dari* on the summit of the *Sûraj-pol*,[2] "his usual custom in the afternoon," and on seeing the object of the *Nai's* eulogy, he ran down into the street, and, catching her skirts, impeded her further progress.

This woman happened to be the same Fortune who had given him dominion, and who had come in this alluring guise to try his virtue, but, as his boldness towards one whom he then regarded as his subject, convinced her of his inability to rule, she withdrew her patronage and likewise the territory of Nadola from Rao Lakhan the Chohân. "But," added the old Brâhman who related the above story to me, "Fortune is always fickle, and a difficult mistress to serve." We learn something of Rao Lakhan from Colonel Tod, in Râjasthân, Vol. I, page 680.

At Nadola are some stone temples and a modest fort: the temples, however, are all comparatively modern, none being older than the fifteenth century of our era; and one cannot help regretting that, in describing these buildings, which are no better than dozens of their kind in Râjpûtâna, Colonel Tod should have thought fit to drag forth for comparisons Cæsar's genius, as displayed in the construction of his bridge over the Rhone, the buildings of the Helvetii, and the earliest

[1] A very ungodlike proceeding truly, and one which, were it practicable, we would abstractly call horse-stealing. But with the Hindûs, might is often regarded as right, and this wonderful arrangement for acquiring a stud is deemed far more glorious than a mere gift.

[2] The "Sun-gate," which yet stands in the town. It is accounted as one of the oldest objects here.

Roman architecture. The comparisons are unnecessarily far-fetched, wholly uncalled for, and serve no other earthly purpose than to acquaint the reader that they are familiar to the author.

Regarding the age of these temples, I found inscriptions at three of them, and these range from 1666-68 to 1744 of the Samvat era.

The inhabitants point to the *Sûraj-pol*, "gateway of the sun," as the oldest building here, saying that it was built by Rao Lakhan, who lived shortly after the last Chohân emperor. The fortress, too, is in all probability old. The present town of Nadola is surrounded by low rubble walls, and has gates, both in the circumvallation and inside, to divide off the different castes and trades into wards or *mohalas*. The houses are built of stone in much the same fashion as those of the trans-Indus country, *i.e.*, shapeless boulders, packed together, with thin shales or wedges of stone inserted horizontally.

There are nine temples within the town, of which four are Vaishnava, two Saivite, and three Jain. The Jaina temples are dedicated to Neminâth, Mahâvira, and Santinâth; the temples of Vishnû are devoted to various incarnations of that deity, and those of Siva contain merely his phallic symbol.

On ascending a fine flight of stone[1] steps, one enters the fort of Nadola from the east, and is confronted by the most handsome temple here. This temple is dedicated to Mahâdêva, and is built of a light-coloured limestone called *sonana*, after a quarry of that name, three *kos* hence. This is the lightest-coloured limestone I have yet seen, and almost resembles white marble.

This temple is richly carved, and contains three inscriptions, each dated in Samvat 1666, and recording the building of the temple from eleemosynary funds. In each corner of a square courtyard, in the midst of which this temple stands, is a small shrine, which is subordinate to the central building; these four shrines are called *Surya-ka-mandar, Devi-ka-mandar*, *Mâtâ-ka-sthan*, and *Sikarband*. From the fortress (whose

[1] This is a very close-grained stone, admirably adapted for building purposes, and called Sozat after a neighbouring quarry.

towers are square) a considerable view of the surrounding country may be obtained. Hence I saw a high conical hill, situated to the west, and crowned by fortifications. I enquired about it from the men who conducted me over the fort, and was given to understand that it was a *burj* or isolated bastion of the main fort, so it must have been used as a "look-out."

Outside the town there are fifteen temples: one of Vokal mâtâ, one of Siva, one of Asapurna mâtâ, two of Hanûmân, one of Rishebâbâ, one of Chatarbhoj, and a ruined pillared temple now called Khetla-ka-sthân.[1] But in many of these are minor shrines, dedicated to various divinities other than, or attendant upon, the principal occupant of the temple, and hence the total number of extramural temples is given at fifteen.

The last-named building is the most remarkable, and certainly the oldest, in Nadola or its neighbourhood. At present only eight massive columns and architrave pieces remain of this ruin, between the pillars of which marriage ceremonies are now conducted; hence its present name.

That these remains represent one of the oldest flat-roofed temples of which we know, no one who has examined them will doubt; and that this building should have escaped the observation of previous visitors to Nadola, is no less surprising than its antiquity is obvious. Originally there were either fifteen or twelve columns in this edifice, as we allow a greater or less number running north and south; east and west no more could have existed than at present, as I observed the outside returns of the architraves where they crown the consols in these directions.

At present, however, only eight columns, each 13′ 3″ high, are *in situ*, and these cover an area 25′ long (east to west) and 14′ 5″ broad (north and south).

The columns rest on massive square bases 5′ 6″ in girth, above which they are octagons of 5′ 1″ girth, and higher still they became cylinders of 4′ 10″ circuit. They are crowned by rudely-hewn capitals, of a style which I will call "four-winged" (the centre portion is circular, and hence their

[1] For a view of which see Plate XIX.

plan cannot strictly be called cruciform, unless it be a Maltese cross), as they send out an angular bracket-like member, which in the case of the outermost ones form supporting consoles, from each face. No traces of sanctum or walls remain here, but much of the materials proper to this ancient temple have been utilised in the construction of a neighbouring shrine in which I found five short incised records, which, from the shape of the stones on which they are cut, I take to belong to the pillared hall just described. On one of the pillars of the Khetla ruins I found a short record in characters of the ninth or tènth century, when the building must have been much in its present ruined condition, as the letters are engraved *outside* the outermost pillar where a wall must have originally stood. The inscription is much obliterated by the action of rain, and only a letter here and there can be made out ; therefore no connected reading can be given here. This remark also applies to the inscribed pieces built into the neighbouring temple; but a few of the characters from their shape appear to belong to the eighth or ninth century A.D.

20.—JÛNA KHÊRA.

Jûna Khêra, or "the ancient ruin," is situated a little to the east of Nadola, on an extensive mound, which is in parts densely covered with fragmentary pottery and burnt bricks. Burnt bricks are somewhat scarce in Mârwâr nowadays, most of the buildings being built either of stone, unburnt bricks simply dried in the sun, or of *ak* (*Calotropis*), a kind of bramble indigenous to these sandy countries. Nevertheless, the bricks in Jûna Khêra are numerous, and large, as I found some pieces almost on the surface 14″ long ;[1] but as none of the pieces which I collected retained two angles entire, I could not determine their width.

On the naturally-elevated plateau called Jûna Khêra, which undoubtedly marks the site of an ancient city, I found

[1] I conclude that the measurement given is the length, for it is at least improbable that it is the mere width, in which case the bricks would become enormously large.

four ruined temples, the foundations of which are formed with large rudely-dressed blocks of stone; in only two cases, however, does anything in the shape of superstructure exist, though in a third building the sanctum screen stands quite alone at the western end of the foundation of its temple, having outlived every trace of walls, &c.

As these ruined temples are disposed over Jûna Khêra almost due north and south, I will describe them in that order, beginning with that building to the north, which is also the best preserved of the four.

Temple No. I is situated almost in the centre of the ruins and retains its deep boldly-carved plinth intact, or nearly so, and also a couple of feet of its walling. This temple stands on an artificially-made rock platform, measuring 124′ east and west, 59′ north and south, and is 8′ 8″ in height above the surrounding fields. Above this again a granite plinth rises for 5′ 9″, and at the highest point the rudely-squared porphyritic blocks, which formed its walls, still retain a mean height of 5′ above the plinth, and hence the present height of this ruin is 19′ 5″ above the fields.

The rock basement, or foundation immediately supporting the plinth, is formed in great part of conglomerate, found on or near to the spot, and measures 29′ 1″ from east to west, and 27′ 6″ from north to south; but the chamber interiorly is only 18′ 8″ by 16′ 4,″ as the walls are very massive.

The entrance to this building was evidently from the east, but the body of the temple is completely filled up with rubbish which has, in course of time, formed a kind of inclined ramp, starting from several feet to east of the building, and leading up to the remains of its back or western wall.

Temple No. II is 105′ long from east to west, 60′ from north to south, and only stands at present 7′ high. This is only a solid mound of massive stones, with traces of walls.

Temple No. III is 48′ 6″ east and west, 40′ 7″ north and south, and 10′ high. This height has reference to the lower portion of the sanctum of the temple (which I have before stated still stands intact, all the other walls having passed away long ago), and on the outside or western face of this sanctum screen I found the figure of a bull, and a few letters incised: the letters are old, but, along with the bull's figure, are very badly cut.

Temple No. IV is 98′ 2″ from east to west, 50′ 6″ from north to south, and 8′ 9″ high.

There is another small ruined building 8′ 9″ long by 10′ 3″ broad, which has walls 2′ 8″ thick, still standing to a height of 4′ 3″.

Of Jûna Khêra nothing is traditionally known, except that it was the first Nadola, and existed previous to the foundation of that town already noticed. It is also stated by the peasants and others with regard to Jûna Khêra, that its inhabitants incurred the displeasure of a certain *Jogî* who cursed the city, thereby transforming it into its present ruinous state, or, as they express it, in their Mârwârî dialect,—The Jogî transformed the Patan, "a standing city," to Datan, "a fallen ruin."

PHILOLOGICAL NOTES.

During my travels in Râjpûtâna, and especially in Mârwâr, I collected the following list of dialectic peculiarities, by conversing with people of various degrees. Each is a distinct impediment of speech, shared equally by the educated and illiterate classes, and no amount of training is capable of correcting it.

Substitute	*for*
h	स *or* श *s* or *ṣ* [1] This impediment confuses 7 with 8 (either pronounced as an ordinal or a numeral); thus, for *sát* (7) the Râjpût will substitute *hát*, which is very like *át* (8).
v which in Mârwâr and Mêwâr is pronounced very clearly	ब व *b* & *v* alike: the former labial is *never* altered.

[1] With the exception of this substitution of *h* for *s* or *ṣ*, al lthese peculiarities appear to have escaped Tod's observation; moreover, he does not remark that the semivowel stands for *ṣ* as well as *s*; he also considers it an impediment proper to Mârwâr; but though it is perhaps more obvious there, I have found it common in several parts of Râjpûtâna. Nor would it be an easy task to locate either of the other five corruptions to any particular part of Râjwâra.

Substitute	*for*
s	च *ch, eg., Chohán* is pronounced *Sohán*.
s	छ *chh* especially in Mêwâr.
z (very soft)	ज *j*, but curiously *jh* is very correctly sounded and undergoes no change.
ó	आ *á* as in *páni* (water), which the *Márwári* calls *poni*.

21.—NÂTHDWÂRA

stands 22 miles north-north-east of Udaipur, and is a town of 5,000 houses built almost concentrically in ranges along the inner edge or bank of a semi-circular rocky ridge which encloses an area of about half a mile from north to south, and is open to the east. But the houses crowd together towards the centre of this crescent, or amphitheatre-like area, and thus the plan of Nâthdwâra would not be unlike a half circle, with its diametrical line to the east.

The granite rocks overlooking Nâthdwâra were originally fortified, and of these fortifications, consisting principally of rough stone walls and dikes thrown across the mountains, portions still exist; the more obvious and best preserved being to the south, above the town. Many of the houses, moreover, are pierced for guns. Nâthdwâra has altogether eleven gates, some of which are both large and handsome, and the town is partially surrounded by low stone walls. But of the eleven gateways, only three large and five small (called *khîrkîs*) are in the outer circumvallation, and three are inside the town and serve to divide it off into compartments, or *mohalas*, in common with several other places which I have seen in Râjpûtána. The large gates are called *Mathura darwaza*, *Thanna darwaza*, and *Lodhighâtî Chamkika darwaza*.

Though the number of houses here is estimated at 5,000, the population is only estimated at 13,000, which only allows about 2½ souls to each dwelling. The population of Nâthdwâra is, however, very fluctuating, owing to the large number of pilgrims whose visits are uncertain, and at the time of my visits (in April 1883), I was given to understand that 1,000 or 1,100 houses maintained for the accommodation of these pilgrims stood empty. The object of attraction here is the great temple of Nâthjî, which is the principal Vaishnav establishment in these regions. It is, however, quite modern, as is everything else here, for the site was formerly an obscure hamlet called *Siarh*, and the temple was built in the reign of Aurangzeb.

The following story of the origin of Nâthdwâra was repeated to me by the people there at least a dozen times, but as Colonel Tod has the popular version in his Râjasthân, Vol. I, page 409, I will quote thence :—

"This is the most celebrated of the fanes of the Hindu Apollo. Its etymology is 'the portal (dwara) of the god' (Nath), of the same import as his more ancient shrine of Dwarica at the 'world's end.'

"Nathdwara is twenty-two miles north-north-east of Oodipur, on the right bank of the Bunas. Although the principal resort of the followers of Vishnu, it has nothing very remarkable in its structure or situation. It owes its celebrity entirely to the image of Krishna, said to be the same that has been worshipped at Mathura ever since his deification, between eleven and twelve hundred years before Christ."

Besides *Nâthjî-ka-Mandar* there are four large temples at Nâthdwâra; three of these are of Vaishnu and one of Siva, as their names will show. They are called *Bal Krishna Ban wârî*, *Vishnû Nâthjî*, *Nonit Lâljî*, and *Sheonâthjî*. There is another group of seven small temples called collectively *sât sarûp*, or the "seven forms" (of Vishnû). The various other shrines at and around Nâthdwâra number fifteen. But there is nothing old at Nâthdwâra, and its establishments. The 4,000 cows, chief mûkhia, pilgrims, and costly offerings, remain to-day much the same as when Tod visited the place, and for further details I would refer the reader to the pages of *Râjasthân*. But I found an old site situate about 3 miles north-east of Nâthdwâra. There is at present a village called Kotragarh built on it, and a portion of the old fort has been utilised for habitations. There are also some old temples at Kotragarh. At Nâthdwâra, the mouth-covered Jains are seen in small numbers, but they have no place of worship here, for there is not a single Jain temple at Nâthdwâra, and I am told they chant and worship in their own dwellings. Tod says (Râj. I, p. 522) that during his visit there were 4,000 cows at Nâthdwâra. There are fewer now; but they are beautiful creatures, and have large spiral horns, which are painted a bright green colour.

22.—CHITORGARH.

My visit to Chitorgarh has enabled me to acquire a mass of inscribed data collected from various parts of that celebrated fortress, and some of these data, along with any remarks, &c., which my examinations called for, have been collected in the present volume. Before proceeding with my own account of Chitorgarh, I will endeavour to give an epitome of the excellent works now before me on the Rock. I need hardly add, the former will necessarily be somewhat brief owing to the fullness and general accuracy of the latter.

The following is from Dr. Stratton's "Chitor and the Mêwâr Family [1]:—

"In approaching Chitor from the west, on which side the Nimach and Nasirabad Railway and high road pass at a distance of 1¼ miles, the road, from either of these, crosses the Gamberi river by a massive old bridge of grey limestone, with ten arches, all of pointed shape except the sixth from the west bank, which is semi-circular. The arched gateways and towers, formerly at either end, have now disappeared. In the first archway from the west is a stone, with an inscription, partly chiselled out; and in the sixth are two, with geometric figures of circles, and inscriptions in vertical lines. These two stones are evidently from older structures and have been cut smaller, regardless of the inscription, and then laid flat, to suit the masonry courses of the pier. The date and builder of the bridge seem not certainly known, as its arching and perfect condition scarcely accord with the popular Hindu idea which refers it to Ari Singh, son of Rana Lakhshman Singh, both of whom were killed in the siege by

[1] Concluding chapter, entitled "Visit to the Fort."

Ala-ud-din in A.D. 1290 or 1303 according to Ferishta's account. Another Mussulman history (not now at hand), ascribes the bridge to Ala-ud-din's son, Khizr Khan, who was for some time left in command, and who called Chitor Khizrabad.

"When Chitor was the living capital of Mewar, the city with its palaces, houses, and markets was up in the fort and the buildings below formed merely an outer bazar. Deserted as it has been for the last three centuries by all that could make it thrive, the modern town is little more than a walled village, with narrow crooked streets. . . . . The town, with its surrounding wall, is situated like an outwork to the lower gate of the principal entrance to the fort close at the western base, and a little north of the middle of the hill, which, as already described, has a north and south measure of between 3 and 4 miles. It is called the Talehti or the *Lower* Town of Chitor, just as at Kalinjar, the village at its base, is known as Tarehti.

"The ascent, which begins from (within) the south-east angle of the town, is nearly a mile to the upper gate, with a slope of about 1 in 15. There are two zig-zag bends, and on three portions thus formed are seven gates, one of which, however, has only the basement left. From the gate at the foot, known as the Padal Pol or Patwan Pol, the first portion runs north for 1,050 yards, passing through the nearly obliterated Bhairo or Phuta (broken) Pol above mentioned, and the Hanuman Pol to the first bend. Here the second portion of 235 yards begins, and turning south at once passes through the Ganesh Pol, and continues to the Jorla Pol, just before the second bend. At this point the third portion of 280 yards, which turns again to the north, commences, and directly after leaving the bend, passes through the Lakhshman Pol, continuing then to the upper or main gate, the Ram Pol. . . . .

"On the second portion of the ascent, a few paces beyond the Ganesh Pol, there is, in the loose stone parapet on the right hand, a fragment of an inscribed stone, about 1¾′ high by 1¼′ broad, the characters on which are old, *i.e.*, much older than those of the inscriptions on the bridge, which are of the ordinary Nagari style. On the upper part of the third portion is a bastion with an old dismounted gun; and at the top facing the great gate, the place of the rampart is occupied by a pillared hall, now used as a guard-house, and apparently of ancient construction, though the spaces between the pillars on the outside towards the plain have at a later date been built up with pointed arches, and these again closed, excepting one, besides which, on the top of a pillar, is an inscription of Samvat 1538 (A.D. 1482) said to record the visit of a Jain dignitary. From the top of this hall, on which there are two four-pillared chhatris, a fine view of the plain is obtained. Outside the Ram Pol are several inscriptions. . . . . There are inscriptions also on stones of the wall itself on both sides of the gateway, one being on the right or south side, and two or three on the left. Sundry of the inscriptions bear the name of Banbir, who was Regent and a would-be usurper about A.D. 1539. Others are merely of Samvat 1832 and 1833, *i.e.*, A.D. 1776 and 1777. The Ram Pol is a large and handsome gateway crowned, not by a true arch, *i.e.*, with voussoirs radiating from a centre, and closed by a keystone, but by a Hindu quasi arch of horizontal courses, in which the upper courses of either side projecting inwards, overlap each other till they meet, or nearly so, being then slabbed over. This is the construction of all the gateways on the ascent, except the Jorla, though in one, the Lachchman, the lower angles of the projecting courses are sloped off, giving the whole the outline of a regular pointed arch.

"Inside the gate, on each side, is a hall or guard-room, supported on square-shaped and slightly tapering antique pillars. Immediately past the hall, on the left hand, a new and wide road, presently to be noticed, has been opened, leading to the north. The *old* road from the gate goes straight on (*i.e.*, eastward) for about 50 paces. Here, directly facing the gate, the hill again rises steeply. . . . .

"At Patta Sing's chabutra the old road divides into three, *viz.*, a steep foot-path in the middle directly ahead, a bridle track more gradually ascending towards the north, and a lane barely passable for a cart to the south. From the Ram Pol thus the visitor has two courses before him : either to thread the old lanes and bye-paths, or to follow the new carriage road. . . . . Then turning south, near a small Hindu temple on the right (west) of the road, it continues in a straight run along the crest, with the old Jain tower standing up grandly in front. The road passes close on the west side of this and the Jain temple immediately on its south. The tower is locally called the *chhota* (or "small") *Kirtham*, this latter being the popular contraction of *Kirtistambh*, or "Tower of Fame,"—*Kirti* meaning fame, strictly speaking, of that sort which is gained by good deeds, as distinguished from the fame of military exploits. Fergusson thus describes it :—

"'One of the most interesting Jaina monuments of the age (the first or great age of Jaina architecture, which extended down to about the year 1300, or perhaps a little after that) is the tower of Sri Allat (Rana Alluji), which still adorns the brow of Chitor.' . . . .

"Of the larger and more modern tower, Fergusson writes :—

"'There seems then to have been a pause, at least in the north of India, but a revival in the fifteenth century, especially under the reign of Khumbha, one of the most powerful of the kings of the Mewar dynasty whose favourite capital was Chitor. His reign extended from 1418 to 1468, and it is to him that we owe the other of the two towers that still adorn the brow of Chitor. This one was erected as a Pillar of Victory to commemorate his victory over Mahmud, of Malwa, in the year 1439. It is therefore in Indian phraseology a *Jaya-stambha*, or Pillar of Victory. . . . . It is nine storeys in height, each of which is distinctly marked on the exterior. A stair in the centre communicates with each and leads to the two upper storeys, which are open, and more ornamental than those below. It is 30 feet wide at the base, and more than 120 feet in height, the whole being covered with architectural ornaments and sculptures to such an extent as to leave no plain parts, while at the same time this mass of decoration is kept so subdued that it in no way interferes either with the outline or the general effect of the pillar.' "

" He remarks in a note: 'The dome that now crowns this tower was substituted for the old dome since I sketched it in 1839. It may be added that the old dome had been injured by lightning, and the repairs were by Maharana Sarup Sing. If the old Jain tower gave the general idea of the newer structure, its ornamental details are Hindu rather than Jain. The stair inside is much wider and easier than in the older tower, and on the interior of the storeys are carved a series of Hindu gods, with the names inscribed below.'

" From either of the two upper open storeys there is a splendid panorama of the hill and the plains below. In the topmost are two slabs[1] (not merely one as mentioned by Tod) with long inscriptions. . . . . From the tower one may turn back a little (*i.e.*, south-west) to the Mahasati and Gaumukh. The Mahasati is a small wooded terrace, a step down, as it were, from the cliff wall which retains the Hathi Kund, and here, before the founding of Udaipur, was the place of incremation of the comparatively few Ranas who died in peace at home; but at that time *chhatris*, or canopied monuments, were either not built or have since been destroyed, as the few now seen are modern, and not those of Ranas.

" Below the Mahasati, on a lower terrace, are the Gaumukhi springs and reservoir. The former are two or three in number, issuing from the cliff face at cow-mouth carvings now mutilated. The water, evidently percolating from the Hathi Kund above, falls first in an old pillared hall, and thence into a masonry reservoir below, eventually, when abundant enough, supplying a little waterfall lower down as already mentioned. . . . . The only three entrances

[1] See plates XX and XXI; and for the inscription in the building at foot of the Tower of Victory, see Plate XXV.

to the fort now are the Ram Pol, the Suraj Pol, and the small gate of Lakha, already described. . . . . Beyond this, on the right, is the *chaugan*, or parade, and farther on, a tank with the Island Palace of Rani Padmini, now being repaired; and, after that, a succession of other tanks. On the western ridge is first passed the large old palace of the Rampura Chief; and, a little farther on, that of Salumbar. Next, on the ridge, is seen the temple of the goddess Kalika Mata, or Devi, the shrine and lower part of which, including the pillars, are said to be older than the present dynasty, *i.e.*, above a thousand years, though repairs to portions have been frequent in later times. Then come close together the ruined palaces of Patta Sing and Jaimal. . . . .

"Midway between magazine and bastion is a carved stone temple now called the Singar-Chauri, containing a canopied masonry daïs, and said to have been built by the Jain Treasurer of Râna Kumbha. The bastion and lofty walls were the commencement of an inner citadel, intended by the usurper Banbir, who ruled in the minority of Udai Sing, to be a protection from foes within Chitor.

"The drive from the Mori Tank hitherto has, to some extent, followed the line of old roads, now improved and made passable, and here it traverses the ruined Moti Bazar. But, farther on, the old tracks turn to the west, where the principal part of the city was, and in the direction of the Ram Pol, while the new drive continues direct to the north, passing on its left the Ratneswar Tank and the palace of Ratna Sing on the farther side, and then, rising out of the valley, mounts the northern loop of the ridge where the new road from the Ram Pol comes up, and from which this circuit of the fort was commenced.

"It was mentioned that the old road from the Ram Pol divided into three at Patta Sing's monument. It is along these lines that most of the commoner parts of the old city may be traced. The one in the middle is merely a steep foot-path leading directly to the higher ground on which the town was mostly built. The one to the north is little more than a bridle-road, but it is worthy of being explored, as it leads to a group of interesting old structures,—*e.g.*, the Kukreswar Temple, the Mataji Kund or reservoir, and the temple of Anupurna Devi or Mata, the shrine of which is very old, though the present temple was built by Rana Hamir Sing in the first part of the fourteenth century. Besides it, is the smaller temple of Ban Mata, and close to the latter is the chhatri of the semi-deified Raghodev, great-grandson of Hamir Sing. In the same direction (south-west) from the tower, but nearer, is a large carved stone temple which Tod notes as built by Rana Kumbha, in honour of his father Mokalji, and dedicated to Brimha; but present local information describes it as built by Mokalji himself. . . . . In the back wall of the sanctum is a huge carved head, showing a full face in front, and a half face at each side, which is perhaps what Tod mentions as a bust of Mokalji. This temple contains two inscribed slabs, one of Samvat 1485, or A.D. 1429, and another much older, and from some other place. A little to the north is a handsome gateway, half built up, known as the Mahasati gate, in a line of wall separating the precincts of the Mahasati and the ancient Mahal or Palace of the Ranas further north. In a panel on the west side is a slab, with a long inscription dated Samvat 1331, or A.D. 1275. Further north and on the parapet is a large temple of Jata Shankar (Mahadeo), from the terrace of which a beautiful view over the lower town and the western plain is obtained. The visits to the foregoing places, traced from the Mahasati to the Jata Shankar Temple, are supposed to be foot excursions from the Tower of Victory; and now returning to it, one may follow the branch road leading to the main drive. At their junction is situated Kumbha's temple known as Kumbh-shyam. It is a huge structure on the west of the drive, and it is dedicated to Vishnu, and by its side is the smaller temple of the Miran Bai, similarly dedicated. Tod describes Miran Bai as the Rani of Kumbha, but local information states she was the Rani of Prince Bhoj Raj, a son of Rana Sanga, the grandson of Kumbha. On the east of the drive, here, is a group of elaborately-carved Jain temples called *Satbis Deorian*, *i.e.*, the 27 shrines. Further north, the Bari Pol, or Great Gate of the old mahal grounds is on the west of the drive. A little way in is another called Tripolia, though there is only one gateway, and beyond this is a third and smaller one. The mahal is in ruins, but evidently was a lofty and spacious building. Traces of blue enamelling on a few spots still remain.

"The drive next passes the eastern end of the Nao Kota Magazine, a hall of massive pillars supporting an arched roof, and now being repaired. This building is at the one extremity of a lofty wall, at the other or west end of which is a huge circular bastion, with vaulted chambers called the Nao Lakha Bhandar, or the Nine Lakh Treasury. . . . .

"There is also at hand a large temple to Vishnu; and not far off, a couple of carved pillars with a cross-bar, where princes have been weighed in gold which was then given to the temples. The road to the south passes between ruins to the Tulja Bhawani Temple built by Banbir, where it forks, the track to the left going to the Moti Bazar on the new drive, and the other to the right continuing past the Nao Lakha bastion and through the old palace to the Tower of Victory. A little off this road and south of the Ram Pol is a bastion with an old brass gun 14 feet long and of 7 inches bore. Tradition has it that several large guns were, at various times, thrown into the Kukreswar Kund, but, as this is deep and the water constant, nothing is certainly known."

I shall supplement the above graphic account with a few extracts from that written by Colonel Tod sixty years before :—

[1]"My heart beat high as I approached the ancient capital of the Seesodias, teeming with reminiscences of glory, which every stone in her giant-like *kangras* (battlements) attested. It was from this side that the imperial hosts under Alla and Akbar advanced to force the descendant of Ram to do homage to their power. . . . . But there was one relic of 'the last day' of Chitor which I visited in this morning's march that will immortalize the field where the greatest monarch that India (perhaps Asia) ever had, erected the green banner of the faith, and pitched his tent, around which his legions were marshalled for the reduction of the city. This still perfect monument is a fine pyramidal column, called by some the *Cherag-din*, and by others *Akbar-ca-dewa*, both having the same meaning, 'Akber's lamp.' It is formed of large blocks of compact limestone, admirably put together, about 35 feet high, each face being 12 feet at the base, and gradually tapering to the summit, where it is between 3 and 4, and on which was placed a huge lamp (*cherag*) that served as a beacon to the foragers, or denoted the imperial headquarters. An interior staircase leads to the top; but although I had the strongest desire to climb the steps, trodden, no doubt, by Akbar's feet, the power was not obedient to the will and I was obliged to continue my journey, passing through the Tulaiti, as they term the lower town of Chitor. Here I got out of my palki, and ventured the ascent, not through one but five gates. . . . . I hastened to my *bechoba*, pitched upon the margin of the Surajcoond, or 'fountain of the sun,' and with the wrecks of ages around me, I abandoned myself to contemplation. I gazed until the sun's last beam fell upon the ringlet of Chitor,[2] illuminating its glory and grief-worn aspect, like a lambent gleam lighting up the face of sorrow.

"Who could look on this lonely, this majestic column, which tells, in language more easy of interpretation than the tablets within, of

'—— deeds which should not pass away,
And names that must not wither,'

[1] Râjasthân, Vol. II, p. 657 (Personal Narrative).

[2] Tod here refers to the Tower of Victory.

and withhold a sigh for its departed glories? But in vain I dipped my pen to embody my thoughts in language; for wherever the eye fell, it filled the mind with images of the past and ideas rushed too tumultuously to be recorded. In this mood I continued for some time, gazing listlessly, until the shades of evening gradually enshrouded the temples, columns, and palaces; and, as I folded up my paper till the morrow, the words of the prophetic bard of Israel came forcibly to my recollection: 'How doth the city sit solitary that was full of people! How is she become a widow! She, that was great among nations, and princess among provinces, how is she become tributary!'

"But not to fatigue the reader with reflections, I will endeavour to give him some idea of these ruins. I begin with the description of Chitor from the Khoman Rasa, now beside me: Chutterkote is the chief amongst eighty-four castles, renowned for strength, the hill on which it stands, rising out of the level plain beneath the tilac on the forehead of *Awini* (the earth). It is within the grasp of no foe, nor can the vassals of its chief know the sentiment of fear. Ganga flows from its summit, and so intricate are its paths of ascent, that, though you might find entrance, there would be no hope of return. Its towers of defence are planted on the rock, nor can their inmates, even in sleep, know alarm.

"Its *kotars* (granaries) are well filled, and its reservoirs, fountains, and wells are overflowing. Ramachandra himself here dwelt twelve years. There are eighty-four bazars, many schools for children, and colleges for every kind of learning; many scribes (*Kyat*) of the Beedur tribe, and the eighteen varieties of artizans." [Here follows an enumerating of all the trees, shrubs, and flowers, within and surrounding the fortress.] "Of all, the Ghelote is sovereign (*dhanni*), served by numerous troops, both horses and foot; and by all the thirty-six tribes of Rajputs, of which he is the ornament (*chatees culan sengar*). The *Khoman Rasa*, or story of Rawat Khoman, was composed in the ninth century; and the poet has not exaggerated: for of all the royal abodes of India, none could compete with Chitor before she became a 'widow.' But we must abandon the *Rasa* for a simple prose description. Chitor is situated on an isolated rock of the same formation as the Pathar, whence it is distant about 3 miles, leaving a fertile valley between, in which are the estates of Beejipur, Gwalior, and part of Beygoo, studded with groves, but all waste through long-continued oppression. The general direction of the rock is from south-south-west to north-north-east; the internal length on the summit being 3 miles and 2 furlongs, and the greatest central breadth 1,200 yards. The circumference of the hill at its base, which is fringed with deep woods, extending to the summit, and in which lurk tigers, deer, hogs, and even lions, is somewhere above 8 miles, and the angle of ascent to its scarped summit about 45°. The *Tulaite*, or lower town, is on the west side, which in some places presents a double scarp, and this side is crowded with splendid objects, the triumphal column, the palaces of Chitrung Mori of Rana Raemul, the huge temple of Rana Mokul, the hundred pinnacles of the acropolis of Gholatos, and last, not least, the mansions of Jeimul and Putto, built on a projecting point, are amongst the most remarkable monuments overlooking the plain. The great length of Chitor and the uniformity of the level crest, detract from its height, which in no part exceeds 400 feet, and that only towards the north. In the centre of the eastern face, at 'the gate of the sun' (*Soorajpol*), it is less than 300 feet, and at the southern extremity the rock is so narrow as to be embraced by an immense demi-lune, commanding the hill called Chitor, not more than 150 yards distant; it is connected with Chitor, but lower, and judiciously left out of its circumvallation. Still it is a weak point, of which the invader has availed himself. . . . .

"Having wandered for two or three days amongst the ruins, I commenced a regular plan of the whole, going to work trigonometrically, and laying down every temple or object that still retained a name or had any tradition attached to it. I then descended with the perambulator and made the circuit.

"The first lateral cut of ascent is in a line due north, and before another angle, you pass through three separate gates; between the last of which, distinctively call the *foota dwara*, or 'broken door,' and the fourth, the *Hanuman pol* (porte), is a spot for ever sacred in the history of Chitor, where its immortal defenders, Jeimul and Putta, met their death. There is a small cenotaph to the memory of the former, while a sacrificial *Jooiarh*, on which is sculptured the effigy of a warrior on horseback, lance in hand, reminds the Seesodia where fell the stripling Chief of Amait. Near these is another cenotaph, a simple dome, supported by light, elegant columns, and covering an altar to the manes of the martyr Rajoode, the deified *putra* of Mewar.

"After passing three more barriers we reach the Rampol, which crowns the whole, and leads into a noble *durri-khaneh*, or 'hall of assembly,' where the princes of Chitor met on grand occasions; and it was in this hall that the genius of Chitor is said to have revealed to Rana Ursi that his glory was departing. On a compartment of the Rampol we found an interdict inscribed by a rebel Bheem of Saloombra, who appears to have been determined to place upon his own head the mor of Chitor so nobly renounced by his ancestor Chonda many centuries before. This was, however, set up when he was yet loyal, and in his sovereign's name as well as his own, 'abolishing forced labour from the townspeople, and likewise dind, or contribution;' concluding with a grant of land to a patriotic carpenter of Gasoonda who had, at his own expense, furnished the Rampol with a new gate. . . . . The next building I came to, as I skirted the western face in a southerly direction, was a small antique temple to Toolsi Bhavani, the divinity of the scribes, adjoining the *Tope-Khaneh Chaoria*, a square for the park, where a few old cannon, the relics of the plunder of Chitor, still remain. The habitation of the *purohits*, or chief priests of Ranas, a plain, commodious, and substantial edifice, was the next; and close by was that of the *Musani*, or master of the horse, with several others of the chief household officers. But the most imposing edifice is that termed *Nolakha Bindar*. This is a small citadel in itself, with massive, lofty walls, and towers built entirely of ancient ruins. Its name would import that it was a receptacle (*bindar*) for treasures, though it is said to have been the residence of the usurper Bunbeer. At the north-eastern corner it has a little temple, richly sculptured, called the Sengar Chaori. From this we pass on to the palace of the Ranas, which, though attributed to Rana Raemul, is of the same character as those of a much higher antiquity. It is plain, capacious, and in excellent taste, the only ornament being its crenated battlements, and gives a good idea of the domestic architecture of the Rajputs long anterior to the intrusion of the Islamite amongst them. The vaulted chamber, the projecting *gokra*, or balcony, and the gentle exterior slope, or *talees* of the walls, lend a character of originality to all those ancient structures of Chitor. . . . . A court-yard surrounds the palace, in which there is a small temple to Deoji, through whose interposition Rana Sanga effected all his conquests. . . . . On leaving the court of Rana Raemal, we reach two immense temples dedicated to the black god of Vrij, one being erected by Rana Khoombo, the other by his celebrated wife, the chief poetess of that age, Meer Bae, to the god of her idolatry, Shamnath. . . . Both these temples are entirely constructed from the wrecks of more ancient shrines, said to have been brought from the ruins of a city of remote antiquity called Nagara, 3 coss northward of Chitor.

. . . .

"We are now in the vicinity of the Kheerut Khamb, the pillar erected by Rana Khoombo on his defeat of the combined armies of Malwa and Guzerat. The only thing in India to compare with this is the Kootub Minar at Delhi; but, though much higher, it is of a very inferior character. This column is 122 feet in height, the breadth of each face at the base is 35 feet, and at the summit, immediately under the cupola, 17 feet. It stands on an ample terrace, 42 feet square. It has nine distinct storeys, with openings at every face of each storey, and all these doors have colonnaded porticos. . . . . It is built chiefly of compact limestone and the quartz rock on which it stands, which takes the highest polish: indeed there are portions possessing the hardness, and exhibiting the fracture, of jasper. It is one mass of sculpture, of which a better idea cannot be conveyed than in the remark of those who dwell about it, that it contains every object known to their mythology. The ninth *Khund*, or 'storey,' which, as I have stated, is 17½ feet square, has numerous columns supporting a vault, in which is sculptured Kanya in the *rasmandala* (celestial sphere), surrounded by the *gopis*, or muses, each holding a musical instrument, and in a dancing attitude. Beneath this is a richly-carved scroll fringed with the *sarus*, the phenicopterors of ornithology. Around this chamber had been arranged, on black marble tablets, the whole genealogy of the Ranas of Chitor; but the Goths have broken or defaced all, save one slab, containing the two following slocas:—

"*Sloca 172*[1]: 'Shaking the earth, the lords of Goojur-khand and Malwa, both the sultans, with armies overwhelming as the ocean, invaded Medpat. Koombkurn reflected lustre on the land: to what point can we exalt his renown? In the midst of the armies of his foe, Khoombo was a tiger, or as a flame in dry forest.'

"*Sloca 183*: 'While the sun continues to warm the earth, so long may the fame of Khoombo Rana endure. While the icy mountains (*hemagir*) of the north rest upon their base, or so long as Himachil is stationary, while ocean continues to form a garland round the neck of Awini (the earth), so long may Khoombo's glory be perpetuated. May the varied history of his sway and the splendour of his dominion last for ever! Seven years had elapsed beyond fifteen hundred when Rana Khoombo placed this ringlet on the forehead of Chitor. Sparkling like the rays of the rising sun, is the torun, rising like the bridegroom of the land.'

"In *Samvat* 1515, the temple of Brimba was founded, and this year, Vrishpatwar (Thursday), the 10th . . . on the immoveable Chutterkote, this Kheerut stambha was finished. What does it resemble, which makes Chitor look down on Meru with derision? Again, what does Chutterkote resemble, from whose summit the fountains are overflowing, the circular diadem on whose crest is beauteous to the

[1] These readings of Tod, which appear to be very free, can now be compared with my photographs of these inscriptions (pp. xxi and xxii).

eye?—abounding in temples to the Almighty, planted with odoriferous trees, to which myriads of bees resort, and where soft zephyrs love to play.

"This immoveable fortress (*Achildoorga*) was formed by the Maha Indra's own hands.

"How many more slocas there may have been, of which this is the 183rd, we can only conjecture, though this would seem to be the winding-up.

. . . .

"On one side of the dell[1] is the subterranean channel called Rani-Bindar, which, it is said, leads to suites of chambers in the rock. This was the scene of the awful johur, on the occasion of Alla sacking Chitor, when the queens perished in the flames; on which the cavern's mouth was closed. Still ascending I visited the edifices named after Jeimul and Putta, and the shrine of Kalka Devi, esteemed one of the most ancient of Chitor, existing since the time of the Mori, the dynasty prior to the Ghelote. But the only inscription I discovered was the following: 'Sambut 1574 Magh (Sudi) 5th and Revati Nikshitra, the stone-cutters Kaloo, Kamir and thirty-six others (whose names are added) enlarged the fountain of the sun (*Suryacoonda*), adjacent to the temple of Kalka Devi.' Thence I passed to the vaulted cenotaph of Chonda, the founder of the Chondawuts, who surrendered his birthright to please his aged sire. A little farther are the mahls of Rana Bheem and Pudmani.

"Beyond this, within a stone enclosure, is the place where the victorious Khoombo confined the King of Malwa; and touching it is the mahl of the Raos of Rampura.

"Further south is a spot of deep interest—the tank and palace of Chitrung Mori, the ancient Puar lord of Chitor. . . . . The interior sides of the tank are divided into sculptured compartments, in very good taste, but not to be compared with the works at Barolli, though doubtless executed under the same family. Being now within 200 yards of the southern bastion, I returned by the mahls of the once vassals of Chitor, *viz.*, Sirdhi, Boondi, Sont, Lunawarra, to the Chaogan, or 'field of Mars,' where the military festival of the Duserra is yet held by the slender garrison of Chitor. Close to it is a noble reservoir of 136 feet in length, 65 feet in width, and 47 in depth. It is lined with immense sculptured masses of masonry, and filled with water. Higher up, and nearly about the centre, is a remarkable square pillar, called the Khourasinsthamba (column). It is 75½ feet in height, 30 feet in diameter at the base, and 15 at the top, and covered with Jain figures. It is very ancient, and I found

[1] Of Gaomukhi.

a fragment of an inscription at its base, which shows that it was dedicated to Adnath, the first of the twenty-four Jain pontiffs :—

"'By Sri Adnath, and the twenty-four Jineswara, Poondarica, Ganesa, Surya, and the nine planets, may you be preserved! Sambut 952 (A.D. 896) Bysak (Sudi) the 30th Gurwar (Thursday).'

"I found also another old inscription near the very antique temple Kookreswar Mahadeo : 'Sambut 811, Magh Sudi 5th Vrishpatwur (Thursday), A.D. 755, Raja Kookreswar erected this temple and excavated the fountain.' There are many Jain inscriptions, but amidst the heaps of ruins I was not fortunate enough to make any important discovery.

. . . .

"Close to the Suraj-pul, or gate, in the centre of the eastern face, is an altar sacred to the manes of Sukeedas, the Chief of the Chondawuts, who fell at his post: the gate of the sun, when the city was sacked by Bahadoor Shah. At the north-western face is a castle complete within itself, the walls and towers of which are of a peculiar form, and denote a high antiquity. This is said to be the ancient place of the Moris and the first Ranas of Chitor."

Regarding Tod's statement that the Jaya Pillar is superior to the Kutb Minâr at Delhi, I think most people who have had an opportunity of comparing them will agree with me in considering that the Jaya Stambha cannot for a moment be classed with the noble monument of Delhi. In describing it as covered with sculptures, Colonel Tod is quite right; but are not spaces judiciously left, far more suggestive of the simplicity which, in architecture especially, lends grandeur to a design?

A too close crowding together of details which cannot be seen from below without binoculars, is, to my mind, architectural impolicy. In effect, the architect of this tower appears to have been unacquainted with the ornate requirements of such a building, and to have fallen into the modern error of covering his work with ornament.

Such ungrateful ineffectual labour is the principal distinction between ancient and modern artistic work in the East. Be the performance embroidery, ornamental weaving in Cashmere wool, silk or gold, incrusting, inlaying, chasing in composition,[1] gold or bronze, architective embellishment, &c., the ancient

[1] Commonly called "Biddrî ware" and now very rare.

master owes quite as much for the beauty of his work, to the unwrought blanks dividing or distributing his design, as to the parts actually worked upon, nor have the former cost the true artist less thought than the latter. The extremely square outlines of the Jaya Kambha are not graceful, and suggest joss-house architecture; indeed, if the too-numerous corners were only a little elevated or turned up in the manner affected at home in Elizabethan times, this monument could pass for one of Chinese construction. The staircase arrangements here are also very peculiar and inconvenient in addition to the entrances and passages being ridiculously low. The design of this staircase has everywhere been made to suit previously inadequate calculations and unthought-out work on the part of the architect. I do not know whether the construction of these steps has yet been described, and probably it has not; hence the following notes.

Broadly speaking, the Jaya Kambha, as seen from outside, has another and smaller addition of itself within. Both the inner and outer shells are divided off into nine storeys, thus forming of the inner portion a complete chamber, and of the outer a quadrangular passage; and it is against the inner walls of these chambers and passages alternately that the staircase is built, so that it is necessary to walk round three angles of the building on arriving at each of the nine landings, and before commencing the next ascent.

Entering from the south, fourteen steps lead from the road to the walled-in platform which runs all round the base of the pillar; from this platform six more steps have to be ascended, and one enters the doorway, in front of which there is a novel arrangement of four steps which lead to the first landing proper. After passing round three angles of the first landing, the staircase is found, and by mounting eleven steps, the second landing is reached; seventeen more steps inside the second chamber lead to the third landing; of these seventeen steps, three must be deducted, as a descent of that number now becomes necessary to reach the quadrangular passage around the third chamber, through three angles of which one is again obliged to thread one's way in search of further steps; these found, fourteen more bring us to the fourth landing, and entering the fourth chamber, ascending sixteen more steps and descending two, the fifth landing, or quadrangular passage round the fifth chamber, is gained. Here the structure has become too narrow to admit of any more staircases inside the chambers formed by the inner column, and hence the ascent from this point is carried on wholly outside these chambers, which remain uselessly empty occupying the room that may have been devoted to wider and more simply arranged steps, by which the journey to the summit of this pillar could be reduced by three fourths. On the fifth landing I found a little outer stone chamber the use of which no one could tell me, and fifteen more corridor steps lead into the sixth landing; sixteen more to the seventh, and fourteen more to the eighth.

On reaching the eighth storey, I found that the staircases which, after many knocks and much labour, had at least borne me, thus far terminated; for here no staircase has been provided at all![1] However, climbing a very rickety wooden ladder, I arrived in the octagonal hall which crowns this edifice. The above gives a total of 127 steps, or, if we deduct the descent of three and two steps, occurring in the third and fifth landings respectively, 122, thus:

Landing.	Steps.	Deductions.	In Corridor.	In Chamber.
I	{ 14 6 4 }	...	1	...
II	11	...	...	1
III	17	3	1	...
IV	14	...	...	1
V	16	2	1	...
VI	15	...	1	...
VII	16	...	1	...
VIII	14	...	1	...
TOTAL . 8	127	5	6	2

[1] I have since heard that there were formerly stone steps here, which have fallen away.

The last chamber, as I have before remarked, is reached by a wooden ladder; but I reckon this ascent as equal to twelve steps of the kind met with in the upper parts of this column, which addition, if allowed, makes the total number of steps in this column 139, or 134, without, or with, the descents, respectively. It is to be regretted that so little attention has been paid by the builders of this pillar to the important matter of lighting. On account of the darkness a greater part of the inside carving (especially the *relievo* tile-work in the walls) is hidden on an ordinarily bright day. I have a list of the apertures, with their sizes, allowed for this column, but it will not be necessary here to give these. Suffice it to say, they are wholly inadequate to the area requiring illumination.

Besides the countless incised labels above and below the images, with which the Jaya Stambha is interiorly embellished (I have taken no note of these further than reading them all, which, however, suffices to show that they are mere names, or attributes, of the deities they mark), I found inscriptions of various lengths, and mostly dated, on the walls of the pillar. These inscriptions—which, according to my information, had been altogether overlooked hitherto, perhaps owing to the extreme darkness before mentioned—I have secured.

But more noteworthy than the above is a discovery which I made of *Arabic inscriptions* in the 3rd and 8th storeys of this pillar. Had these inscriptions been *incised* in the manner common to Hindî records, I should not attach much importance to their discovery; but they are beautifully carved in *high relief,* and careful examination convinces me that they are no additions, and that their execution was *coëval with the building of the pillar.* These inscriptions only consist of the word *Allah* (الله), repeated nine times on the pillarette bands or entablatures of the storey, and eight times on those of the eighth storey. But they are so carved from the body of the chamber pillarettes as to form an essential part of their design, and these pillarettes are, again, part and parcel of the entire building. Identical with them in workmanship, along with these remarkable little columns, the inscriptions have received the same high polish as the remaining portions of the structure! What could be more conclusive of Muhammadan influence in the erection of the Pillar of Victory?

The word *Allah* is tantamount to the Musalmân *Kalmeh*, and indeed is often considered an efficient abridgment of the whole creed. Here, then, we have in the midst of countless idols, the very ideal of unity and anti-idolatry. This discovery opens up a problem, of which the only solution which presents itself to me is, that the barrier dividing the Hindus and Muhammadans three centuries ago, was far less impassable than it is at the present day: the numerous marriages between Râjpûts and Mughals during the Empire will, I think, support this assumption. We know that Akbar the Great had decided leanings towards Hindûism, and it is not impossible that the opposite process may occasionally have taken effect in the Hindû conscience.[1]

I also examined the Jain Pillar called the *Kirtam*, or *Chhota Kirtam* as it is commonly called to distinguish it from the larger column above described, and being the name by which it is most generally known, I will use it to designate this tower, which is believed to have been erected as an act of "piety" or "penance" (*Kirat*+*Stumbha*, "a pillar," shortened to *Kirtam*). Although the larger tower is often called the *burra Kirtam*, or "great Kirtam," this name is but the vulgar and wrong one, for the correct name is *Jaya* or *Jait-stambha*, "Pillar of Victory."

The *Kirat* monument has been pronounced by competent authority to be a *Jaina* building, and it certainly exhibits full-length standing male figures which are depicted with long arms, curly hair, and many of the characteristics by which, in the present state of our knowledge, we recognise Jain figures. But much of the ornamental work is of the conventional type common to the Brâhmanical and other Hindû styles of design. The execution of these sculptures, however, seemed to me to be somewhat superior to that employed on those on the later and larger "Pillar of Victory."

[1] For a view of the Tower of Victory, see Plate XXII.

There are, in the *Chota Kirtam*, sixty-nine steps altogether,—*i.e.*, fifty inside the column, and nineteen by which the large platform upon which it stands is reached. A careful examination of this building convinces me that it is absolutely unsafe, and the authorities will prevent a catastrophe happening sooner or later, by taking steps to forbid pilgrims and others from ascending or entering it. The whole building is considerably out of the perpendicular, and the walls inside bulge out in several places in a most alarming manner. In addition to this, some of the small columns which are supposed to support the roof of the bow-window-like arrangements used as seats, lean in all directions and support nothing. It is needless to mention that the north side of the topmost storey has long since fallen away, carrying with it nearly one third of this chamber.

While on the subject of the present condition of these monuments, I may here mention that on touching a supporting pillar on the top (9th) storey of the large tower (Jaya-Stambha) it swung backwards and forwards, and on trying some others they were found equally loose. Now, as the stone could not have shrunk, I conclude that some other part of which we are unaware must have given way, lifting the weight of the roof, which originally rested on these pillars, off its legitimate support.

On overturning the stones, &c., at the foot of the *Kirtam* (Jain tower), which are the remains of the northern part of its top chamber, I found among the *débris* a fragmentary inscription in one line. The principal value of this inscription rests in its unquestionable association with the monument, and the form of the letters may assist in determining finally its age: the letters are certainly older than those of the two stelæ in the 9th storey of the *Jait lât*.

Amongst the temples on the Chitor Rock, perhaps the most excellent examples are those called *Mokal-jî-ke-mendar*[2] in the precincts of the Pillar of Victory, and the graceful and richly-carved little building called *Singâr-Chaurî*[1] or *Vêdî.*

[1] See Plate XXIII. [2] See Plate XXIV.

The general plan of the first-named temple is a large hall forming the body of the building, to the east of which is a small, square, cell-like, dark chamber; the former being roofed in by the usual overlapping slabs which are reduced from a square base to a circular acme forming a conical dome exteriorly, the spring of which rests upon four fine pillars. Behind or to the east of this dome rises an obeliscal spire (*sikar*) of the usual kind. This spire is, however, much broken, and its original height could not well have been less than 50 feet.

On three sides of the building, *i.e.*, west, north, and south, there are three porticos from either of which the temple can be entered; but the main entrance is from that to the west, which is joined by a fine flight of steps.

The dimensions of the temple of Mokal are as follows:—

		Ft.	In.
	Principal Chamber.		
	Interior measurement from east to west	33	6
	" " " north to south	31	4
	Thickness of walls	3	3
	Smaller Chamber, or Sanctum.		
Square.	Interior measurement east and west	13	3
Square.	" " north and south	13	3
Square.	Thickness of walls	4	5
	Entrance Porch (west).		
	East and west, including steps	13	2
	Two minor porches (north and south).		
	East and west, inclusive of steps	11	6
	Space between dome supporting pillars (called bedî).		
	East and west	15	6
	North and south	15	6

From the above it becomes apparent that the extreme outside length of this temple is 72′ 3″ (east and west), allowing for the thickness of walls in the sanctum and central hall, and its extreme outside breadth, including porches and thickness of walls, 60′ 10″ north and south.

The square cell at the eastern end of this building is very dark, and contains a colossal triform statue with hands. The faces of this sculpture, which bear a placid and dignified expression, are well proportioned and finely wrought, and they have the long, split ears generally attributed to effigies of Bûddha. I caused this image to be lighted by torches which were absolutely necessary to a proper inspection of it in the brightest and hottest of April days. It struck me as a curious circumstance that this building being almost intact (the *sikri* or spire alone having fallen in, by which accident we have more light than was originally admitted), this remarkable colossus should be enveloped in such gloom. I have on more than one occasion seen the finest tracery work and sculpture thus completely hidden by the exigencies of their architectural surroundings, but never so large an image as this colossal *tria juncta in uno* of the Indians.

After a building has been dismantled, speculations innumerable are permissible, and indeed common, as to how it was originally lighted. But the temple of Mokalji is almost intact.

When questioned, the people of Chitor informed me that they had been always under the impression that whenever Râna Mokal or other princes of Mêwâr visited the temple, the image was *specially* illuminated.

The temple of Mokal at Chitor is full of carvings, and the ceiling of its central hall is tastefully sculptured in bands of fruit, flowers, pûja-bells, and figures of human beings and the lower animals. But by far the finest sculptures in this or indeed any other temple on the Chitor Rock, are sixteen bas-reliefs carved on octagonal bands of the eastern pair of pillars which support the domed ceiling of the *Mahamandapa* or great hall—the western pair being quite plain.

In describing the sculptures on these two pillars, I will in both cases commence with their western faces, as these look towards the main entrance, and are, therefore, best lighted.[1]

[1] I tried to photograph some of these sculptures ; but the chamber in which theyoccur is far too dark, and several plates were wasted in the attempt.

South Pillar.

The first scene here depicts five human figures, of which two are large and three small: one of the former represents a woman carrying a water-jar on her head, and a man standing before her with hands joined in an attitude of adoration. The minor figures are much broken. This sculpture, along with the others of this set, is remarkable for the elaborate detail and technical excellence of its workmanship, the woman's hair being most minutely delineated.

The second scene, also, has five figures, and I understand it to represent the passing of judgment by the elders on two criminals. Here are the standing figures of the elders and the executioner holding two crouching figures by the hair of their heads, as though awaiting the verdict.

The third carving is very well modelled and proportioned, and depicts two standing figures, male and female. The former holds in his left hand a stiletto, apparently with a view to commit some rash act—perhaps suicide—and turns away his face from the female, who grasps the armed hand and obviously dissuades him from his purpose. Two mystical human hands wave above the man's head; these may possibly be meant for the *akashvani* or "heavenly voice" or influence. The whole design is most effectively—indeed dramatically—conceived.

The fourth scene shews two female figures in supplicatory attitudes.

The fifth scene is filled with vigorous action, and consists of a musical festival; six male figures play six musical instruments, *all* of which are in frequent use at the present day, though some are found in a slightly altered form. The figure in the upright corner beats a drum (*dhol*) with all his might; the next figure plays two bells (ornamented); a third figure is seen clashing together a pair of cymbals (*khasâla*); a fourth (in the right lower corner) has a timbrel-like kettle-drum (*daf* or *nakâra*); a fifth figure is semi-nude and seen in back view quite full, so that the instrument in this case is invisible; the sixth and last figure of this interesting group is seen full to the front, blowing a flute (*mûralî* or *bansî*) in a very animated posture as though he were dancing.

The sixth scene is similar to the fourth.

The seventh scene represents a group of two standing figures, male and female, respectively. The former is bearded, and the latter holds in her hand a branch of a tree, possibly as an emblem of fecundity.

The eighth scene is similar to the fourth and sixth.

North Pillar.

The first scene on this pillar has seven figures, of which four are standing and three are seated. With the exception of two figures much mutilated, and one in the centre of the composition, gracefully holding a lute, all are praying.

The second scene presents a male figure carrying a long sword, and embracing a female with an infant in her arms, while a small child plays with the infant. It is possible that this scene may have been designed to convey the idea of the return of a warrior from battle to the bosom of his family.

The third scene has six figures in three tiers or storeys, the topmost row representing a laughing and bearded man holding in his hands some indistinct object which he shews to a woman. The other four figures, one of which is armed, appear to be engaged in cooking at a caldron or camp kettle. I take this for a camp scene.

The fourth scene presents a group of seven females in various attitudes. Of these, the central figure holds a vase and is a fine type of Oriental beauty.

The fifth and sixth are much mutilated, though they contain some spirited female figures.

The seventh scene is in all probability the most interesting of the whole series, and in its half a dozen figures gives us both a duel and an execution. The upper pair of men fight with shields and sabres, and their armour, accoutrements, &c., even to the knobs or bosses on their shields, are most carefully delineated, and shew that the manufacture of these articles has altered as little during the last eight centuries as that of the musical instruments figured elsewhere. The lower portions of this comprehensive and instructive scene shews a pair of kneeling figures bound hand and foot, while an executioner holds his knife to the neck of the male figure to our left; but the female with him may possibly be a mere witness, though it is pretty clear from the general distribution of action in this trio that she awaits her turn for immolation.

The eighth scene has five male figures, four presenting wreaths, while a fifth, seated on his haunches, pours a water oblation over a phallas.

The *Singâr-Chaurî* or *Vêdî* may be described as a square building with four wings projecting from its four sides. The main or central chamber of the *Singâr-Chaurî* measures 22′ internally both ways, *i.e.*, from north to south and from east to west, the building facing as nearly as possible the cardinal points, and is entered from the west. Western entrances, though elsewhere generally rare in Hindû temples, which are commonly entered from the east, are very common in the temples at Chitor. The above dimensions of the *Singâr-Chaurî* are increased by the four wings or niches before mentioned, two of which (those to the east and south) form separate chambers as they have no outlets.[1] The niches to the north and west, on the other hand, have door-ways, the former being a minor and the latter the principal entrance to these temples, consequently the two niches merely form porches.

Notwithstanding the differences of construction, these recesses are uniformly 7′ deep by 9′ wide, and as the walls throughout the building are 3′ 3″ thick, we will arrive at the total exterior dimensions by the following multiples:—

Length and breadth	22′	
Recess	7′	
Ditto	7′	
Thickness of wall	3′	3″
Ditto	3	3″
TOTAL .	44′	6″

[1] These chambered niches have false floors, *kûrsî*, which can be used for seats 3′ 2″ high.

The total height of this building with its dome is about equal to its total length and width. But I have reason to believe the dome is a modern addition, and that it is not part of the original building, which was most probably a flat-topped one—1st, because this dome is badly formed and rudely built of rubble and lime mortar; 2nd, because it is the only member of this building composed of these materials, the temple being otherwise of solid stone richly carved; and 3rd, because it does not suit and disagrees with the building generally. Therefore the height of the *Singâr Chausirî* in its original form was probably not over 30 feet.

In the centre of this building, and raised 4′ 1″ from its floor, is a forty-two-sided and highly ornamental *vêdî*, or altar, which supports four carved pillars each 7′ high and bearing lintels 1′ 3″ deep; thus the total height of the *vêdî* is 8′ 9. This *vêdî* is at present uncovered, save by the cupola of the temple itself, and the area between its pillars is 9 square feet.

I found several inscriptions in this most interesting building, of which four are incised on three angles of the entrance pilasters, and the remainder were found about the *vêdî*.

The wall of a temporary fort erected by the would-be rebel Banbir, unfortunately runs right across this temple externally, thus in a measure bisecting the building and obstructing the view of it as a whole. A fair idea of the temple can, however, be obtained by viewing it from the south-west corner.

23.—NIMTOR.

On the road which connects Nîmach and Jhâlrapatan, and about 3½ marches from the former place, I found an old site in close proximity to which there now stands a small hamlet called Nimtor—perhaps an abbreviation of *Nimtola* or *Nimthor*.

Nimtor possesses three temples, one of which is an early Brâhmanical shrine and stands somewhat apart and about 500 paces distant from the inhabited portion of Nimtor, though within its immediate precincts, as it is frequently visited by the villagers. On the right-hand side of this temple and above its doorway, which faces due east, I found an inscription of seven lines and dated in Samvat 1027, or A.D. 970.

There is a rudely sculptured, though well proportioned, life-size stone bull (*Nanda*), which the sculptor has depicted in a seated posture. At present it faces this temple. The peasants have a tradition that originally the temple descended from heaven, and that before visiting the earth, it moved from place to place, and finally took up its present position at Nimtor. The sculptured *Nanda*, according to the Nimtor people's belief, was also itinerant, though its wanderings were often carried into different paths than those followed by the temple, so that the temple arrived in Nimtor long before the *Nanda* ("bull"), which is said to have come from Gûzrât.

From the above curious folk-tale, I infer that the large image of the bull is not coëval with the temple, but of somewhat later date; and indeed this was the conclusion which I arrived at on first seeing the figure, the minute elaboration of whose trappings seemed to me comparatively modern.

The temple, on the other hand, is certainly quite one thousand years old, and, though small, of a very graceful exterior.

The door uprights and lintels are beautifully carved in dark-coloured limestone, and a roof constructed of over-lapping slabs of stone in the usual manner of such buildings, results in a circular cupola inside and semi-spherical dome outside. I observed some excellent sculptures (bas-reliefs) let into the back and side walls of this temple, which do not appear to have belonged to the original building.

Inside the Nimtor temple there is a large lingam of Mahâdêva, on the four sides of which are sculptured human faces, so that the whole forms a *chaumûkhî*. A water-vessel is suspended above the lingam, and to this day emits a fine stream of clear water as an oblation to Siva. In the temple of Nimtor I found an inscription which is, however, in bad preservation.

24.—JHÂLRAPATAN OR CHANDRAVATI.

The present city of Jhâlrapatan is of very modern formation, and its name was originally simply *patan*, "a city," and it is said that *Jhâla* or *Jhâlra* is the racial name prefixed by the ruling family of *Jhâlas*. I am inclined to accept this derivation of the present name in preference to that assigned for it by Tod and other writers, *i.e.*, "the city of bells," the popular tradition of the former existence of 108 temples with bells notwithstanding. If these bell-temples were one hundred and eight in number, it is clear that they could not have stood within the area of the present city of Jhâlrapatan, though they may have existed on the old site on the banks of the Chandrabhaga river, nearly a mile distant to the south-east, for there alone could so many temples stand. At present there are thirteen temples at Chandravati.

The walled-in city of Jhâlrapatan possesses only a small number of comparatively modern temples and no traces of earlier ones.

Finally, if the word *Jhâlrapatan*, in its literal sense of "city of bells," ever did designate a city, it is a unique coincidence that the race who rule here should be known by a name so very similar.

The position chosen for the modern city of Jhâlrapatan, as being so entirely separated from the old and excellently situated Chandravati, caused me some surprise, and affords one more example of the gradual decadence of the preference formerly shewn by the founders of ancient towns for the banks of rivers on which to build. The advantages to a city by such close proximity to a river are not unmixed, but in India especially such a position is on the whole preferable from general considerations.

As Chandravati is by far the most interesting spot in this neighbourhood from an antiquarian point of view, I will endeavour to describe the remains here before proceeding to the neighbouring modern city of Jhâlrapatan.

The earliest group here is that formed by the celebrated pillared lingam temple of *Sital-eswar Mahâdêva*, and the two smaller ones (apparently a pair) behind or to the west of it. Of the first of these, only the front (east) pillared hall or porch remains intact, or nearly so;[1] the back (western) portion, in cluding the sanctum, has been entirely demolished and since

[1] Tod calls this pillared hall of the Mahâdêva temple at Chandravati the "Sengar Chaori," with what object I fail to perceive.

rudely rebuilt with mortar; fragmentary figure-sculptures, ornate carvings, and even entire pillars from the same building or from others (I rather think these pillars are more modern than the temple into which they have been built, and that therefore they do not belong to it), have been built into these restorations, in many cases flush with the outside mortar surface, and in all quite at random and without arrangement. The disproportionately massive mortar roof above the original hall is also clearly a modern addition. For a view of this unhappy and heterogeneous attempt at restoration, see Plate XXVI.

Dimensions of Temple of Sital-eswar Mahâdêva.

Entire length (outside) from east to west . . .	64′ 4″
Original pillared hall „ „ . . .	27′ 4″
Mortar and débris restoration (modern) east and west	37′ 0″
Entire width (outside) north and south . . .	33′ 9″
Total number of pillars in original hall . . .	30′ 0″
Height „ „ „ . . .	10′ each.
Circumference „ „ „ . . .	5′ 9″
Thickness of fragmentary remains of original wall near entrance to sanctum of temple . . .	3′ 0″
General height of temple	30′ 0″
Central space in clear court betwixt the innermost rows of pillars (transept) east and west . .	12′ 4″
Central space in clear court betwixt the innermost rows of pillars (transept) north and south . .	11′ 7″
Space between pillars forming the double row around the above central court extreme eastern and western aisles	6′ 2″
Space between pillars forming the double row around the above central court extreme northern and southern aisles	5′ 7″
Space between pillars forming the double row around the above court (both rows alike) . . .	3′ 2″

I found an inscription of two lines in this temple on the screen-wall. The inscription is much damaged and was completely covered and filled up with lime; but I am hopeful that the style of the letters may be useful in finding the age of the temple.

The carvings in the temple of *Sital-eswar Mâhadêva* are superb, more especially the foliated work in the second and third ceiling panels (counting from the sanctum) of the northern row: these two panels exhibit four different strata, as it were, of minutely sculptured ornamentation, on the *same slab of stone.* These are the only examples of such *deeply* carved work on stone which I have seen, and must have cost infinitely more pains to produce than mere sculptures in the round, for the sculptor must have found it a difficult task indeed to wield his chisel in the deeper recesses without chipping or in other ways defacing the projecting work. Every space in the ceiling of this hall was formerly embellished with such panels; and it is surprising that these two have been suffered to remain unharmed by the spoilers, who are variously called Ghores and Mughals, Shahabuddin and Aurangzeb.

I may add that the carvings at Chandravati struck me as being of finer texture and generally superior to those found in any other part of Râjpûtâna.

The second and third temples of this early trio are very much alike in the matter of size and general appearance, and differ principally in the style of the pillars supporting their respective porches, the pillars of one being of spiral form, and those of the other having geometrical forms carved on them. Perhaps the sharpest and finest carvings at Chandravati are exhibited on these two little *mindras*, whose floors are raised considerably from the ground. The temples were formerly approached by steps which have long since disappeared.

Both are linga edifices dedicated to Siva; that furthest to the south is 19′ 6″ in length east and west, and 17′ 8″ in width north and south and 20′ 6″ in height from the ground-level. The thickness of its walls throughout is 2′ 6″, and the height of a *Vajrahâsan* inside is 5′. The corresponding temple furthest to the north and abreast of the above-mentioned building is—

Length (east and west) . . .	16′ 3″
Width (north and south) . .	19′ 0″
Height from ground . . .	20′ 1″
Thickness of walls . . .	2′ 3″ throughout.
Height of kûrsî . . .	4′ 6″

About 100 feet distant from the above group of temples stands the flat-roofed temple which is called by the people *Har Sishi Mâtâ-ke Mindar*. But this name is doubtless erroneous, the statues in and about the temple being certainly Vaishnava in character.[1]

I secured a photograph of this temple, and also of an inscribed pillar in front of its porch, and measured it with the following results :—

Length (east and west)	30′ 6″
Width (north and south)	22′ 2″
Height	15′ 0″
Thickness of walls	3′ 7″

It possesses two sculptured pillars in front of the porch, one of which is inscribed with old letters.

The following are a few of Mr. Fergusson's remarks on the temple of Chandravati,[2] which I described in the opening part of this account, and for a view of which see Plate XXVI :—

"Among the more complete examples, the oldest I know of, and consequently the most beautiful, is the porch or temple at Chandravati, near Jhâlrapatan, in Râjpûtâna. In its neighbourhood Colonel Tod found an inscription, [3] dated A.D. 691, which at one time I thought might have been taken from this temple, and consequently might give its date, which would fairly agree with the style [4] judged from that of some of the caves at Ellora, which it very much resembles. As recent discoveries,[5] however, have forced us to carry their dates further back by at least a century, it is probable that this too must go back to about the year 600, or thereabouts. Indeed, with the Charori in the Mokundra pass, and the pillars at Erun, this Chandravati fragment completes the list of all we at present can feel sure of having been erected before the dark ages. There may be others, and if so,

[1] In the plan by General Cunningham (Arch. Report, Vol. II, Pl. LXXV) this temple is called Kâlika Devi.

[2] History of Indian and Eastern Architecture, Chap. IV, pp. 448-491.

[3] "Tod's Annals of Râjasthân, Vol. II, p. 734."

[4] "Picturesque Illustrations of Ancient Architecture in Hindostan, Pl. 6, with description.—*General Cunningham.*"

[5] "Archæological Reports, Vol. II, p. 264, agree with me as to the date &c."

it would be well they were examined, for this is certainly one of the most elegant specimens of architecture in India. It has not the poetry of arrangement of the Jaina octagonal domes, but it approaches very nearly to them by the large square space in the centre, which was covered by the most elegantly designed and most exquisitely carved roof known to exist anywhere. Its arrangement is evidently borrowed from that of Buddhist Viharas, and it differs from them in style because their interiors were always plastered and painted; here, on the contrary, everything is honestly carved in stone."[1]

Before taking leave of Chandravati, I will quote a happy and brief account of the old site from the facile pen of Colonel Tod (Râjasthân, Vol. I, p. 638):—

"The sites of temples mark the course of the stream for a considerable distance, the banks being strewed with ruins. Flights of steps forming ghats reach to the water's edge, where multitudes of gods, goddesses, and demons are piled, and some of the more perfect placed upon altars of clay, around which some lazy well-fed gosens loiter, basking in the sun."

The following description of the city proper was compiled by Major H. B. Abbott, the Political Superintendent of the State of Jhallawâr. It appears in the account of Jhallawâr in the Râjpûtâna Gazetteer, Vol. II, page 206; the account of the *chhauni* in which the Chief of Jhallawâr and the Superintendent reside, is due to the same reliable authority.

"The old town of Jhâlrapatan lay a little to the south of the modern site along the banks of the Chandravakâ stream, which is now a few furlongs from the centre of the new town. The name is said by Tod to mean the 'city of bells,' as the old town, being a place of some sanctity, contained 108 temples with bells to correspond. It was also known from its position by the name of Chandravati Nagrī. This city was destroyed and its temple despoiled in the time of Arungzeb; all that was left of the ancient place in 1796 was the temple of *Sat-Seheli*, or 'seven damsels' (still standing in the new town), and a few Bhil huts around it. In that year Zalim Sing founded the present city, removing the tahsil from Urmal to Jhâlrapatan, and building a city wall."

[1] "Tod (*loc. cit.*) gives several plates of the details of the porch by a native artist—fairly well drawn, but wanting shadow to render them intelligible."

25.—MOKAND-DWÂRA

Is situated 30 miles to the north-west of Jhalrapatan.

Mokand-dwâra, or "the Darra" as it is generally called,[1] is possessed of two old and now ruined temples. The village or hamlet of Mokand-dwâra is accessible from the south through an artificially-formed pass which is hewn out of the rocks, and fashioned into a regular gateway which can be opened and closed at pleasure.

The mountainous range in which this little outlet is cut can be crossed elsewhere only with great difficulty, and hence I am inclined to regard the post as a strong one. This was the scene of General Monson's battle with, and retreat from, the Maharatha forces headed by Yeswant Rao Holkar.

Mokand-dwâra is at present a small hamlet of about twenty-five dwellings, but quite four times as great an area as is inhabited is in ruins. The deadly nature of the water here is held accountable for this decrease of population.

Of the two early temples at Mokand-dwára, one is called *Bhîm-ke-chaurî*, or "*Bhîm's* Nuptial Hall." This temple is remarkable chiefly on account of its lintels and consoles, being elaborately carved *all over* with strange animal forms and floral scrolls. The temple of *Bhîm* measures 21′ 7″ to the extreme limits of its pillars (exterior dimension), but as the foundation lies very irregularly, it is impracticable to arrive at the precise height, for the elevation of the original floor is left uncertain by the incomplete number of bases; the greater part of the floor having been burrowed into by wild animals—principally the pig, I understand.

I found a short inscription deeply incised on one of the pillars of this temple, which, with a slight variation, is repeated on the neighbouring temple which is nameless.

The inscription on the temple of *Bhîm-ke-chaurî* is as follows:—

अ चंपंत भतज जो गी ।

a chanpat bha taj Jogi (?)

[1] So common has the latter name become that I could not get the natives to understand the former. They all called the place Darra, and professed ignorance as to the whereabouts, or, indeed, the existence of Mokand-dwâra

and is probably a religious pilgrim's proper name with the title of *Jogi*, "devotee," added thereto.

The temple is said to be incomplete, and to have ever been so, and the following local folk-tale which seeks at once to explain its apparent incompleteness, and its name of *Bhîm-ke-chaurî*, attaches to it :—

Bhîm Singh, one of the Panch Pandû brothers, fascinated by his bravery one of the *Devis*, or goddesses, who, in consequence of her attachment, desired to be united to him, and therefore instructed him to build in a single night a suitable nuptial hall (*chaurî* [1]) in which to celebrate their marriage ceremony. But though Bhîm Singh tried to build the place, as instructed by the goddess, in one night, he failed to do so, and the cock, "the harbinger of morn," crowed ere it was ready, thus breaking the spell by which the building was to be built, *i.e.*, secrecy and nocturnal labour; for it is a superstitious belief that the gods (*devatas*) can perform their miracles only by night: and so it came to pass that in the morning the building was abandoned in an incomplete state, and the marriage was postponed.

The second building, which I shall call the nameless temple, stands in close proximity to that of Bhîm Pandû, and appears to be somewhat older than it. Indeed, I have heard from General Cunningham regarding this temple, that it has been deemed to be as old as Asoka's time. But I have seen similar niches to those which figure on the pillars of this temple, on temples of much later date.

The length of this temple is 20′ 4″, and the two inscriptions which I found on its pillars are as follows:—

अ चपं त ध्य ज ।

achanpat (*or achapant*) *dhaj.*

छ ण यि क मो चो रै ।

chh n ye kame cho rai.

[1] Chauri, as the name implies, is "a square place" or platform in the centre of a building, around which reeds are stuck into the ground at equal distances. The bride and bridegroom walk round the Chauri seven times when they are married. I found traces of such a Chauri in the centre of this temple.

These letters are comparatively modern if we except the ch (>) which is seen in inscriptions of the eighth and ninth centuries A.D. They are, therefore, not of any importance. But no others exist on these buildings.

When I first arrived at Mokand-dwâra, I thought that the name of that place may have been derived from the deified Krishna, and that it was, therefore, synonymous with *Nâth-dwâra, Thâkûr-dwâra*, &c., as all these prefixes are epithets of Vishnu. But I was given to understand that the village (though much larger than it is at present) was founded by one Mahâ Rao Mokand Singh, who gave his name to the village.

The palace (*mahal*) of Abla-Mînî at Mokand-dwâra was also built by this chief, Mahâ Rao Mokand Singh, for Abla Mînî, a very beautiful girl whom the Mahâ Rao discovered at a village ten miles hence, called Khairâbâd, where she was born and brought up. The girl's name was Abla, and she was called Mînî on account of her being of the aboriginal tribe of Mînas; and it is said she would only consent to leave her father on the condition that a suitable palace be built on a mountain, so that her father could see her residence from Khairâbad in the day-time. Moreover, that he might not lose sight of it even by night, she desired a lamp to be lighted on the summit of the mountain every night.

This lamp is still lighted in the upper chamber of the palace once a year, in memory of the beautiful Abla Mînî, in whose praise several songs are locally sung by the peasantry. The only other object here worthy of notice is the building called *Bâra-dwâra*, and consequently having twelve doors.

It was built by the Mahâ Rao Râm Singh, and is situated on the summit of the high-peaked hill to the east of, and quite near to, that on which the mahal of Abla Mînî stands. It is occasionally used by the chiefs as a shooting-box.

Both the temples with which I opened this brief account of Mokand-dwâra, stand together in a somewhat jungly plateau, and together cover an area of 59′ 6″ by 14′.

Mr. Fergusson in his "History of Indian and Eastern Architecture," Chapter IV, page 448, writing of Central and Northern India, remarks that "at Erun, in the Saugor territory, are some fragments of columns and several sculptures that seem to belong to the flourishing age of the Gûptas, say about A.D. 450, and in the Mokundra Pass there are the remains of a choultrie that may be as old, or older, but it is a mere fragment,[1] and has no inscription upon it."[2]

The bases of the pillars in Bhîm's Chaurî are 5″, the shafts of the pillars 6′ 4″, the capitals 1′ 3″, the architraves (which are richly carved) also 1′ 3″, and the consoles 1′ 5″ in height. The circumference of the pillars is 5′ 10″.

The height of the pillars of the second temple is almost identical with that of the first, and they are in several other respects very similar; hence they were taken for a single temple, though in reality they are distinct buildings, belonging moreover to different periods.

The principal architectural antiquities in the Kota State[3] are those of Râmgarh, about 60 miles to the east of Kota.

Râmgarh appears on the map as close to a semi-circular system of rocks which form the rim of a basin or valley, and it is in this valley, and at a very small village, called Srînagar, that certain antiquities described to me as beautifully-carved stone temples, figures, &c., are situated.

Kishan Bilâs was also mentioned as possessed of some exquisitely-sculptured temples.

The capital of the State (Kota) possesses some fine buildings, both religious and secular, and the palace of the ruling chief has a most imposing external appearance, owing principally to its being considerably higher than the other buildings *intra muros.* It is a large but very straggling building, which appears to have been added to at almost every successive

[1] A view of these remains may be seen in Mr. Fergusson's "Picturesque Illustrations of Indian Architecture," Plate 5. But he omits to mention that there are *two distinct temples*.

[2] It will have been observed that I discovered three inscriptions here.

[3] I am indebted for this information to Major C. A. Baylay, the able Political Agent of Kota, and regret much my inability to visit Râmgarh. But I had been instructed to examine Bhimgaj and Ranthambhor, so selected a northward road as the quickest by which those places could be reached, the camping season being already unusually advanced.

reign. Its foundation is much higher than the ground-level of the city, and is therefore approached by *jampans*,[1] or *tom-jons* as the Kota folk call them.

26.—KHATKAR-BHIMGAJ.

Remains of sorts stretch for nearly 4 miles north-east of the village of Khatkar, the oldest being along the southern brow of the high mountain which runs from the village to the Mej river.

It is most probable that this site was occupied long before the present village was built, and abandoned on the advent westwards of the river, the tortuous windings of whose branches have subdivided the site into countless hillocks, and all is now overgrown with brushwood and dense *jangal*.

There are, however, three well-preserved, though comparatively modern, stone temples situated to the south and south-west of the present village of Khatkar; here, also the early remains before mentioned continue their course.

The largest of these temples is elaborately carved and dedicated to *Thâkûrjî*, from which I understand it to be a temple of Vishnu. It is 60′ high, 139′ in circuit, and stands upon a base or platform, 8′ 8″ in height, 84′ 3″ in length (east and west), and 56′ 4″ in width (north and south). There are eighteen carved pillars, each 9′ 9″ high, supporting the dome of the outer hall, or the *ardhamandapa*, which affords an area of 16′ 3″ inside for loungers and devotees to rest in. The platform on which this temple stands is approached by twelve steps, and six more lead to the sanctum, over which rises a tall dome or truncated *sikrî*. The walls of this temple are generally 2′ 3½″ in thickness.

The second is a Jain temple dedicated to *Parswanâth*, and is said to have been built by a *banya*. It measures 21′ 2″ square, and is a little higher than the temple of *Thâkûrjî* before described.

The enclosure or courtyard in which this temple stands is 51′ long by 21′ 2″ (the breadth of the temple) broad.

[1] A conveyance much resembling a sedan chair.

The third temple at Khatkar is a Vaishnava structure, and measures 37′ long, inclusive of its front pillars (which are 20 in number and each 7′ high), and 13 feet broad.

This little temple stands on a platform 7′ high, and is approached by eight steps. The interior area or space afforded by the above dimensions, after allowing for pillared porch wall, &c., is 11′ 8″ both ways.

The first and third temples face the west, and the second (Jain temple) faces the east.

The only lingam temple I could find in this neighbourhood is situated on a high hill to the north of the village of Khatkar.

Amongst the rocks about half a mile to the north-east of Khatkar are two temples, a *tir-dawâlî*[1] or rest-house for pilgrims, and in one of these temples I found an inscription dated in Samvat 1716. Here also is a *gopha* or rock-cut passage entered by a *khirki* or wicket, 3 feet high; but the passage increases inside to 8′ or 10′ feet in several places, and leads, according to local belief, to a village called Pâli, about 20 miles east of Khatkar.

27.—BHIMGAJ.

Bhimgaj is a small *tola* of 11 dwellings and 40 inhabitants. It stands in the open plain, which is formed of a deep clayey loam, cut up into several *nalas* to the north-east of Khatkar, from which place it is about $2\frac{3}{4}$ miles distant.

There are three rocks which skirt Bhimgaj in a triangular fashion, and as I searched these very carefully in quest of an inscription which I heard existed here, I may now add their exact positions. There are no more rocks near Bhimgaj. The first rock bears north by west of Bhimgaj, the second due south, and the third south-east; but the nearest of these is $1\frac{1}{2}$ miles from the hamlet.

The only inscription which I could find is at the base of a *chhatri* about half-way up the last-named mountain, which is very high and precipitous. But the inscription is quite mo-

[1] From *tir*, "three," and *dawâl*, "a wall," *i.e.*, a building composed of three walls, and hence almost entirely open on one side where the roof is often supported on pillars.

dern, and several days' search, besides offres of rewards to the wood-cutters, failed to find any others in this neighbourhood.

The small village of Bhimgaj was founded about 30 years ago by Râjâ Bhim Singh, who used to come to these parts on hunting expeditions. The inscribed *chhatri* bears on its summit a lingam of Mahâdêva, together with its accompanying *nandi*, or "bull." It is called *Mahâdêva Dharamnâth.*

I regret now that I did not go to Râmgarh, for the inscription among the rocks of Bhimgaj is not old as I was in hopes it would turn out.

Amongst the rocks through which the Mej river has cut its way, I observed a *band* (" dam") of solid dry work, which must have been called for shortly after the advent of this stream towards Khatkar. It was but a quiet rivulet while I was at Khatkar, but I believe it is a mountain torrent shortly after the rains.

In the mountains to the south of Bhimgaj I found four other temples perched up in positions that to my mind seemed not altogether safe. They are small and modern, and therefore unworthy of further description.

INDEX.

P

R

S

PILLAR OF FIRÚZ TUGHLAK.

Photo-Collotype, Survey of India Offices, Calcutta, February 1887.

INSCRIPTION IN IDGAH.

Lithographed at the Survey of India Offices, Calcutta, January 1887.

HUMÁYUN MOSQUE.

Photo-Lithographed at the Survey of India Offices, Calcutta, February 1887.

TOMB OF SAIYED SHÁH.

Lithographed at the Survey of India Offices, Calcutta, December 1886.

TOMB OF ALI TAJAREH.

Lithographed at the Survey of India Offices, Calcutta, December 1886.

TOMB OF KUTBS.

Photo-Lithographed at the Survey of India Offices, Calcutta, November 1886.

Zincographed at the Survey of India Offices, Calcutta.

Site of Rock inscription shewn thus +

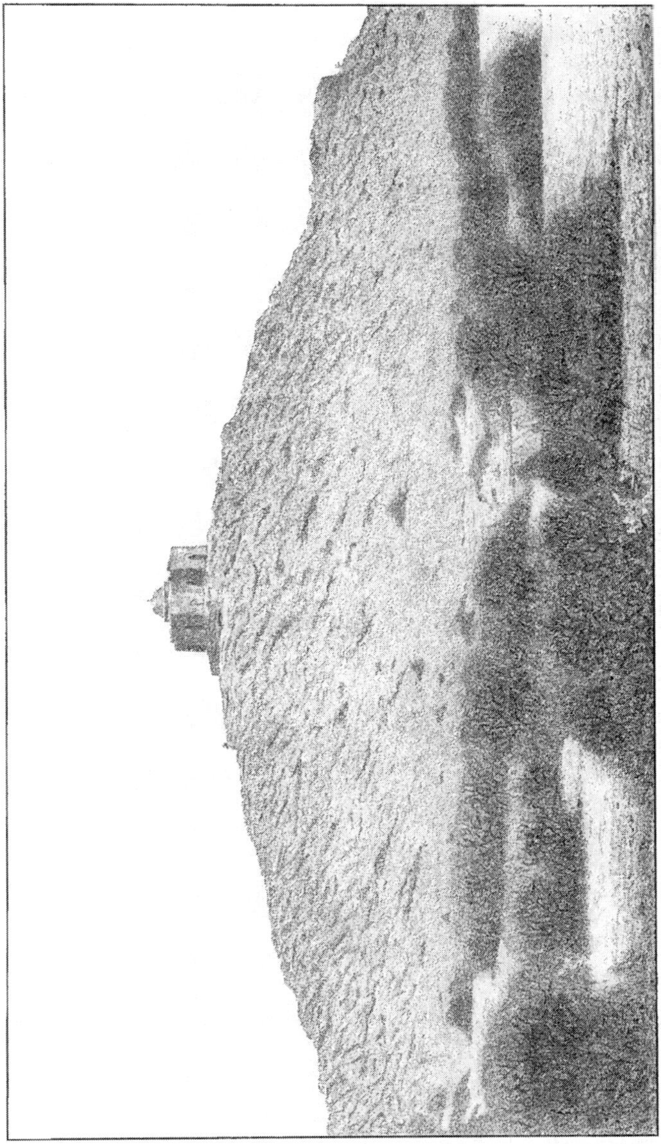

PRITHI RÁJÁ'S KACHERI.

Lithographed at the Survey of India Offices, Calcutta, November 1886.

S. E. CLOISTER - TOWER OF GREAT MOSQUE.

Lithographed at the Survey of India Offices, Calcutta, December 1886.

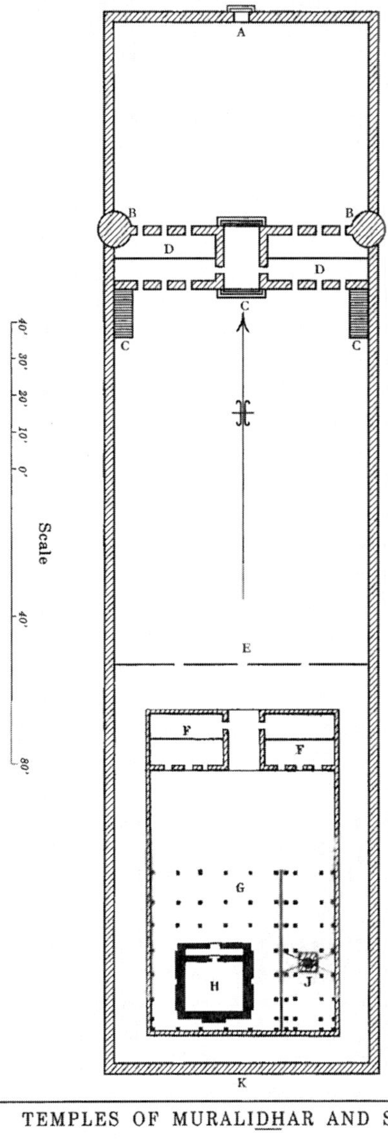

REFERENCES.

A. Main entrance.

B.B. Minarets

C.C.C. Gallery steps.

D.D. 1st Gallery.

E. Partition.

F.F. 2nd Gallery.

G. Pillared Court of Temple.

H. Temple of Muralidhar.

J. " Siva.

K. Circumvallation.

TEMPLES OF MURALIDHAR AND SIVA.

Lithographed at the Survey of India Offices, Calcutta, December 1886.

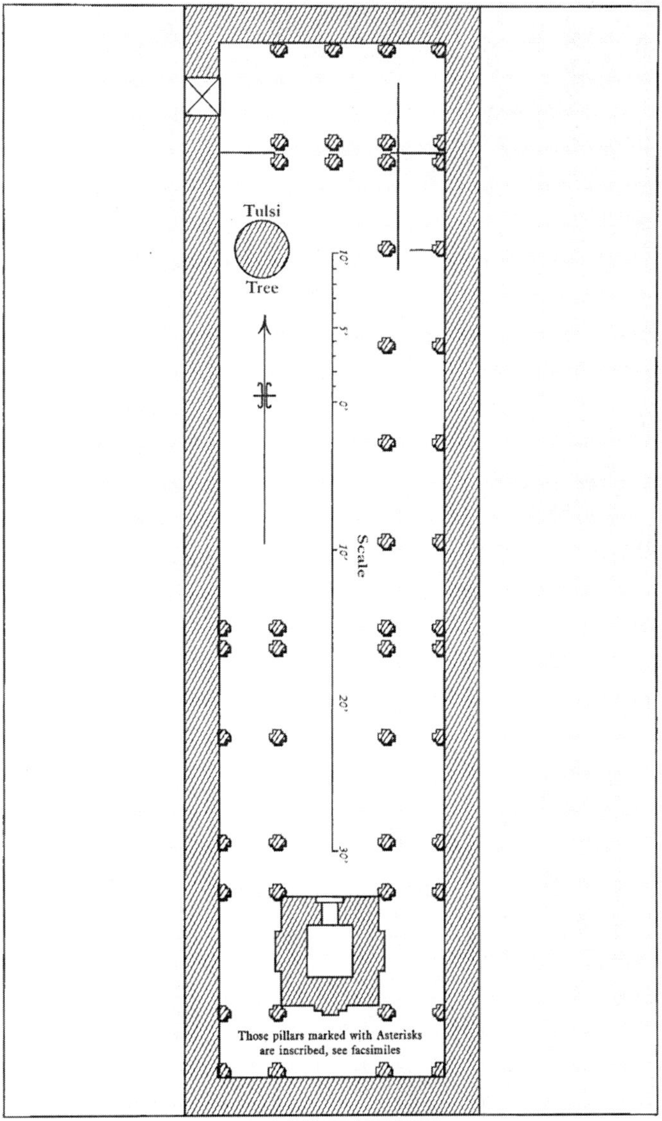

BARMAYAN TEMPLE.

Lithographed at the Survey of India Offices, Calcutta, December 1886.

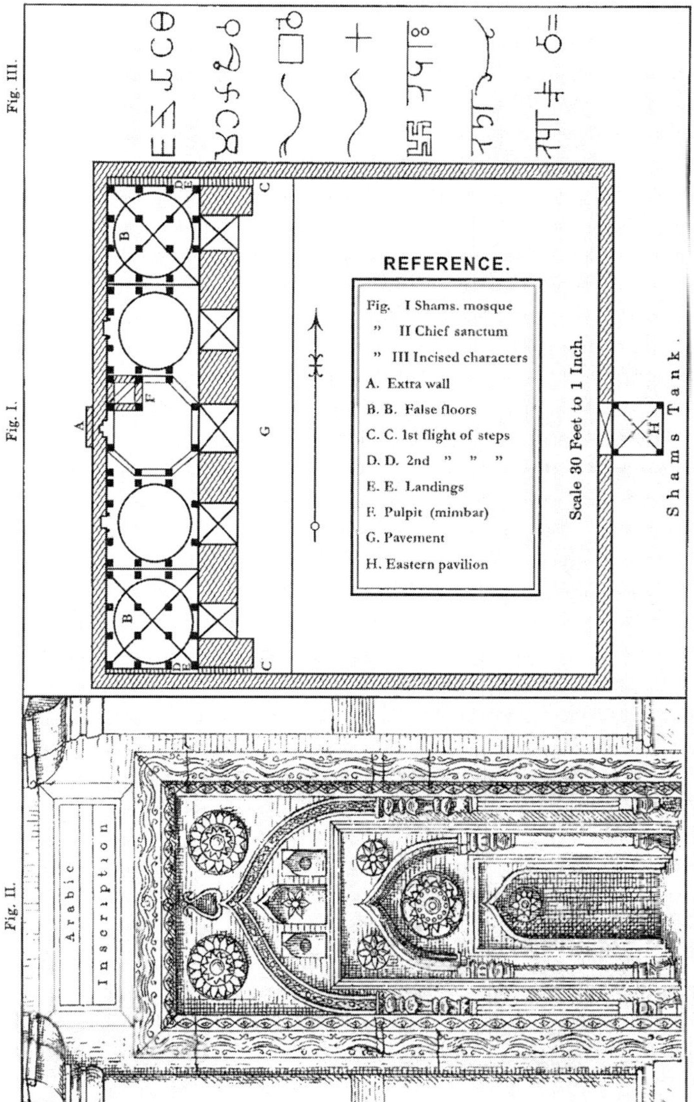

Lithographed at the Survey of India Offices, Calcutta, December 1886.

GATEWAY OF ATARKIN.

Lithographed at the Survey of India Offices, Calcutta, January 1887.

CENOTAPH OF RIO GANGA.

(Side View).

Photo-Collotype, Survey of India Offices, Calcutta, February 1887.

CENOTAPH OF RIO GANGA.
(Front View).

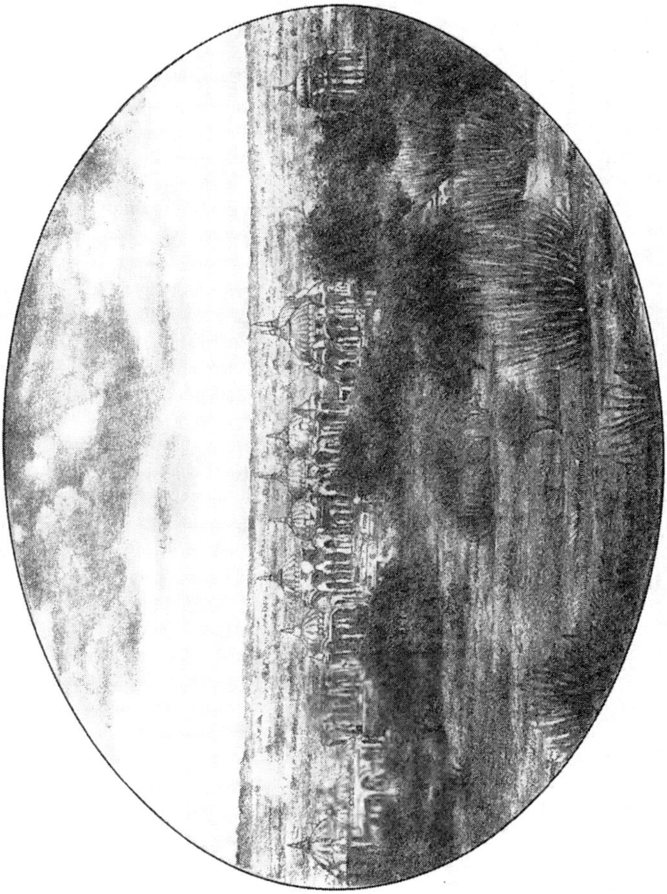

CENOTAPHS OF MARWÁR QUEENS.

Lithographed at the Survey of India Offices, Calcutta, January 1887.

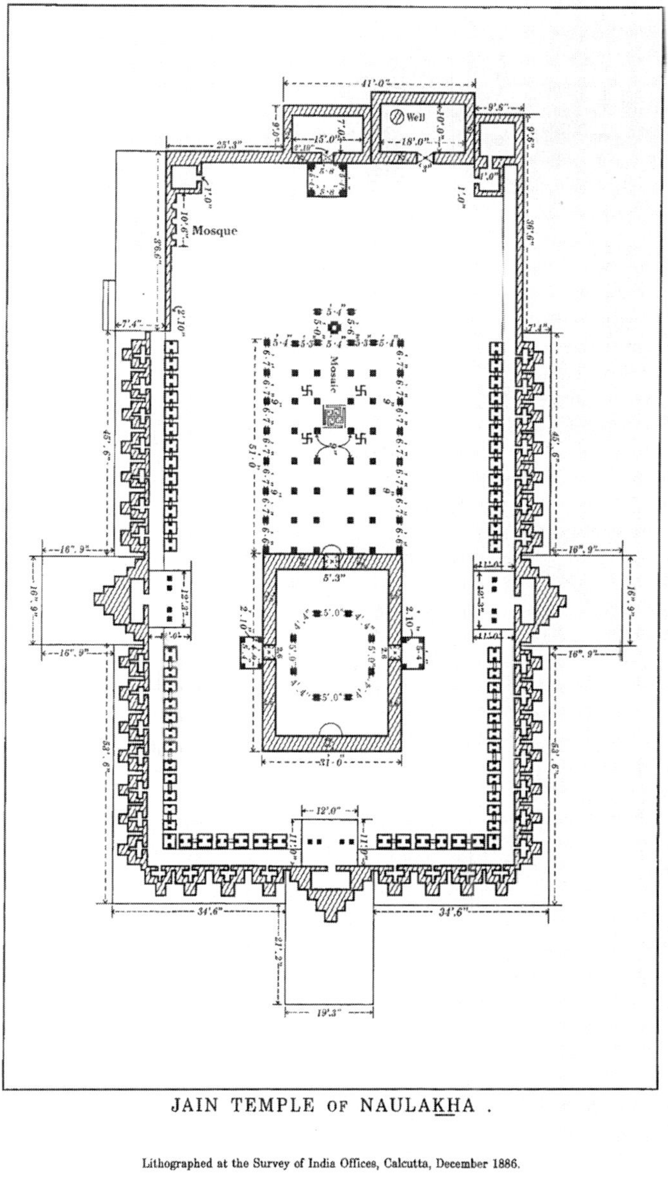

JAIN TEMPLE OF NAULAKHA.

Lithographed at the Survey of India Offices, Calcutta, December 1886.

KHETLA STHÂN RUINS.

Lithographed at the Survey of India Offices, Calcutta, November 1886.

INSCRIPTION AT FOOT OF TOWER OF VICTORY.

Lithographed at the Survey of India Offices, Calcutta, December 1886.

No. 1-INSCRIPTION IN NINTH STORY OF PILLAR OF VICTORY.

Photo-Collotype, Survey of India Offices, Calcutta, January 1887.

No. 2-INSCRIPTION IN NINTH STORY OF PILLAR OF VICTORY.

Photo-Collotype, Survey of India Offices, Calcutta, January 1887.

THE PILLAR OF VICTORY.

Lithographed at the Survey of India Offices, Calcutta, February 1887.

TEMPLE OF MOKALJI.

Lithographed at the Survey of India Offices, Calcutta, January 1887.

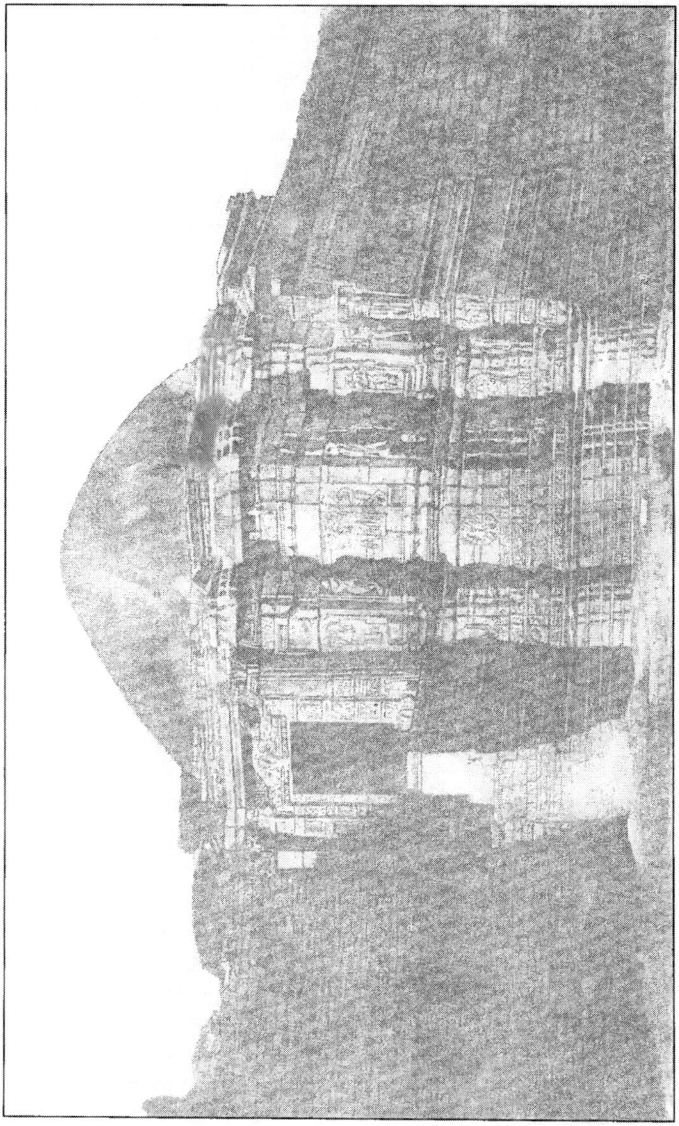

SINGÁR CHAURI.

Lithographed at the Survey of India Offices, Calcutta, December 1886.

ORIGINAL PORTION OF CHANDRAVATI TEMPLE.

Lithographed at the Survey of India Offices, Calcutta, December 1886.

GUPTA INSCRIPTION FOUND IN HAJI RATTAN'S TOMB.

Photo-Collotype, Survey of India Offices, Calcutta, August 1887.